Bass Fretboard Basics

by Paul Farnen

ISBN 978-0-7935-8195-5

Visit Hal Leonard Online at
www.halleonard.com

Contact us:
Hal Leonard
7777 West Bluemound Road
Milwaukee, WI 53213
Email: info@halleonard.com

In Europe, contact:
Hal Leonard Europe Limited
42 Wigmore Street
Marylebone, London, W1U 2RN
Email: info@halleonardeurope.com

In Australia, contact:
Hal Leonard Australia Pty. Ltd.
4 Lentara Court
Cheltenham, Victoria, 3192 Australia
Email: info@halleonard.com.au

Table of Contents

Background

Most Western music revolves around scales and chords. For this reason it is important to first learn the *components* of scales and chords—that is, notes and the intervals (distances) between them.

Range

The range of pitches playable on the four-string (standard) bass as well as the extended ranges of the five- and six-string bass are shown below in relation to a standard piano keyboard (88 keys). In this instance, the *actual* sounding pitches are written on the staff. (Normally, music for bass is written one octave higher than it actually sounds.)

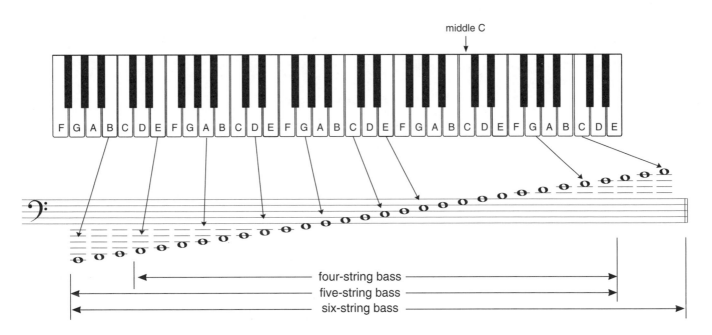

Note Names

The name of each note or *pitch* is taken from one of the first seven letters of the alphabet: A, B, C, D, E, F, or G. Additionally, pitches may lie between these letter names. These are identified with sharp or flat signs—a *sharp* sign (♯) raises the pitch of a note one half step (the equivalent of one fret) and a *flat* sign (♭) lowers the pitch of a note one half-step.

There are two pairs of letter-named notes that do not have an extra pitch between them. They are *B and C*, and *E and F*. These pairs of notes are found on the piano keyboard wherever two white keys lay side by side (with no intervening black key). These notepairs are referred to as consecutive half steps.

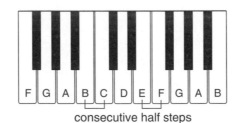

consecutive half steps

Chapter 1

Tuning

The standard tuning for both acoustic and electric bass is shown on the fretboard diagrams below.

Four-String Bass:

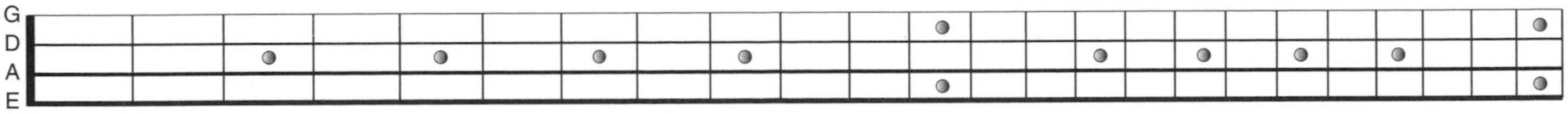

Five-String Bass:

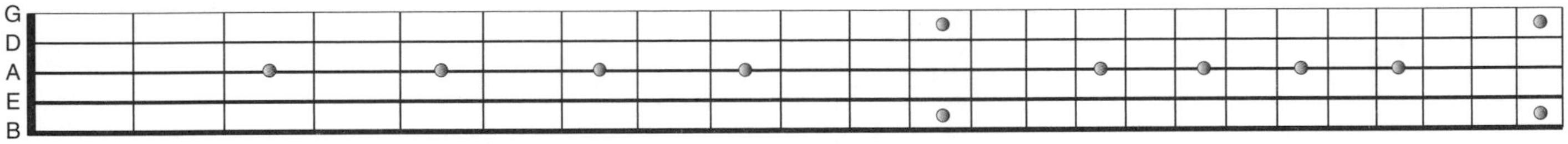

Six-String Bass:

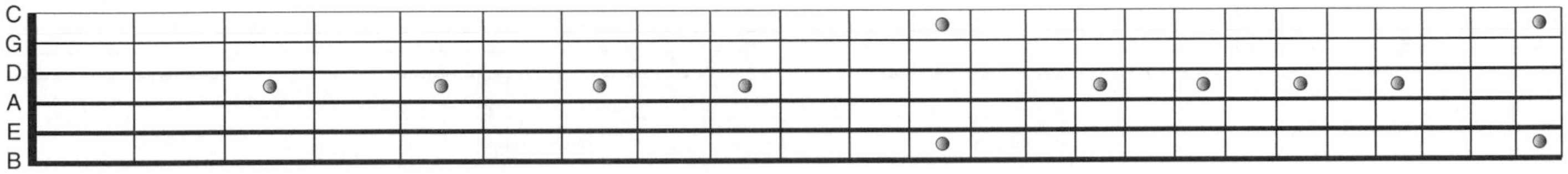

Notice on all of the diagrams above that the letter names of each string are four letters apart. The bass is said to be tuned in *fourths.* This method of tuning gives the player the best access to the most notes with a minimal amount of hand movement. Other tunings are possible, but less common.

1 2 3 4   1 2 3 4   1 2 3 4

B C D **E** F G **A** B C **D** E F **G** A B **C**

1 2 3 4   1 2 3 4

The Natural Notes

The first fretboard diagram below shows the locations of all the natural notes (no sharps or flats) on the four-string bass. Since the five- and six-string fretboards contain all these plus an additional string or strings, only the notes of those additional strings are shown.

Four-String Bass:

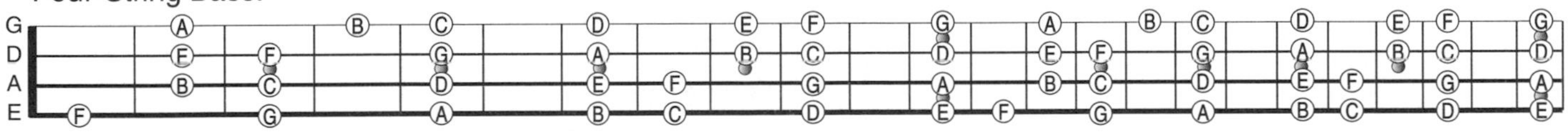

Five-String Bass:

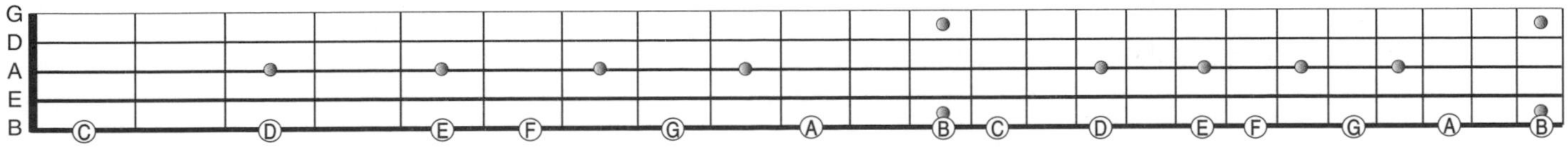

Six-String Bass:

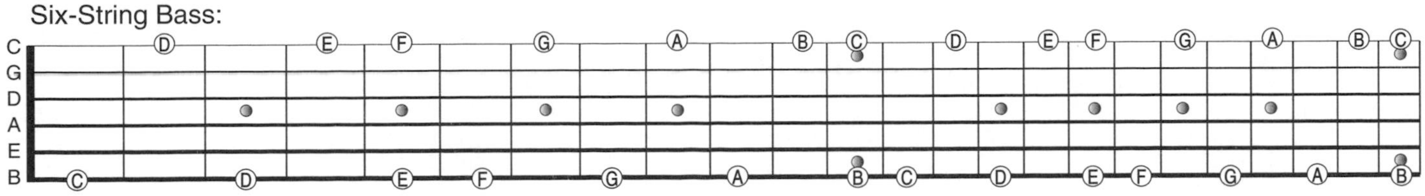

Whole and Half Steps

A *whole step* is a distance of two frets. Any two notes with a one-fret space in between them are a whole step apart. A *half step* is a distance of one fret. Any adjacent notes on one string are a half step apart. The following diagrams illustrate two ways that whole and half steps can appear on the fretboard.

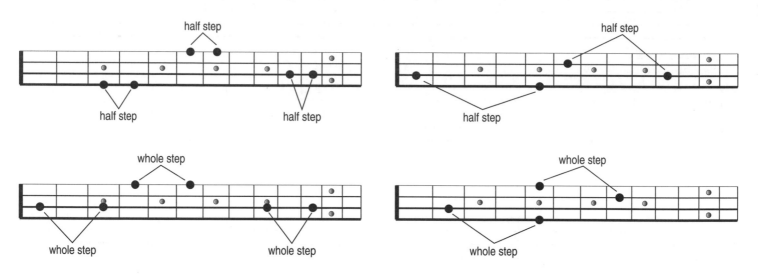

Interval Names

An *interval* is the distance between two notes. Whole and half steps are types of intervals. A whole step is also known as an interval of a *major second.* A half step is also known as an interval of a *minor second.*

Intervals retain their names whether they are *ascending* (the second note is higher than the first) or *descending* (the second note is lower than the first).

Summary

- The names of the notes in music are taken from the first seven letters of the alphabet.

- The bass is tuned in fourths (whether four-string, five-string, or six-string).

- Naturally occuring half steps are located between the notes B–C and E–F.

- Two notes that lie next to one another on a string make up a half step.

- Two notes that are two half steps apart, or two frets, make up a whole step.

- A major second is the interval name of a whole step.

- A minor second is the interval name of a half step.

The Major Scale

2

Background

The *major scale* lies at the heart of nearly all music in the Western world. It has shaped the kinds of instruments we play and the music we make. Because of this heritage, it is logical we begin by creating the major scale and learning how to play it.

All scales are created by assembling intervals (usually whole and half steps) into some kind of order. The major scale sounds "major" due to its arrangement of whole and half steps.

Building the C Major Scale

The diagram below shows the major scale on one string, in this case beginning on the note C. Notice the sequence of whole and half steps. This is known as the major scale's *interval formula.* This same sequence will be used to construct the major scale in *any* key (from any starting pitch).

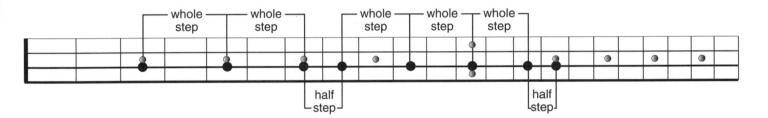

The next diagram shows that the major scale is composed of seven different pitches (eight including the octave) and that each note has a different letter name attached to it. Below, the same scale is shown in notes and TAB. (TAB reflects a standard four-string bass.)

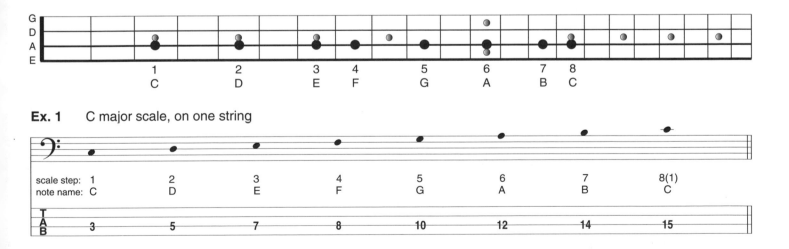

Ex. 1   C major scale, on one string

7

Common Fingering Patterns

Here, the major scale appears in a pattern that moves across the neck on three strings. Notice that the number and name of each note is exactly the same as before.

The fingering used to play the scale is notated in the diagram. This particular pattern is undoubtedly the most common and familiar to bass players. It will be used extensively in this course and will be referred to as "second-finger diatonic" because the second finger of the fretting hand plays the root of the scale (which in this case is a diatonic major scale).

fingering:
G
D
A
E
1
1
2
2
3
4
4
4

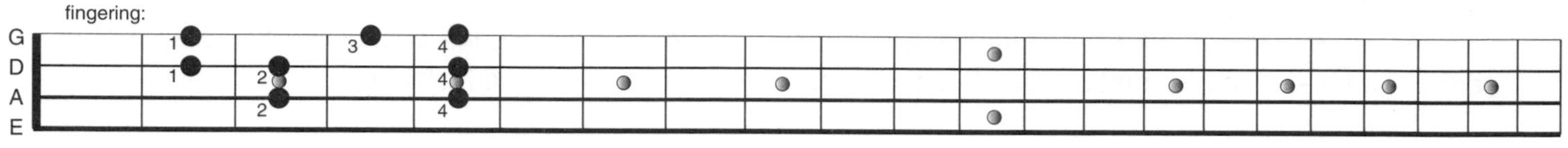

Ex. 2 C major scale, second-finger diatonic

scale step: 1 2 3 4 5 6 7 8(1)
note name: C D E F G A B C
T
A
B
3 5 2 3 5 2 4 5

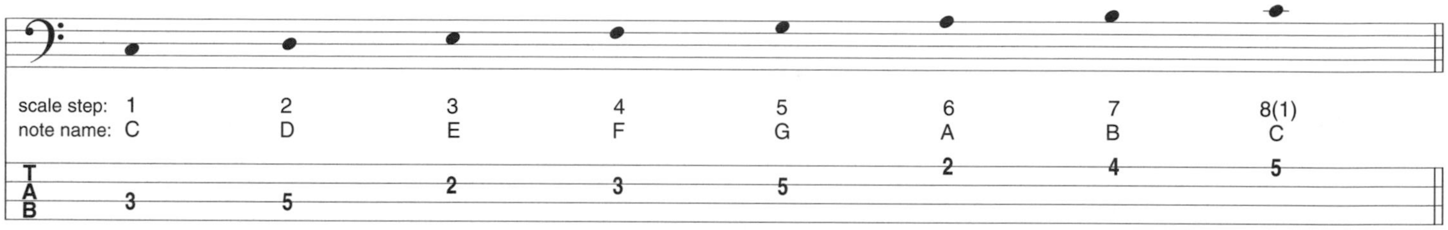

Another fingering pattern for these same notes of C major begins with the fourth finger playing the root note. This fingering will be referred to as "Fourth Finger Diatonic." It contains a shift of fret-hand position (down a fret) to play the last two notes on the G string.

fingering:
G
D
A
E
1
2
1
1
3
3
4
4

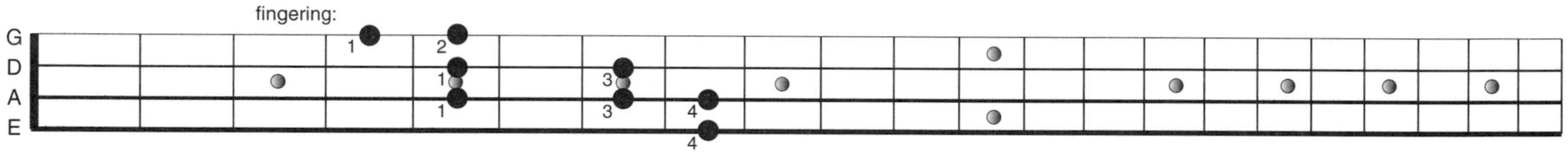

Ex. 3 C major scale, fourth-finger diatonic

scale step: 1 2 3 4 5 6 7 8(1)
note name: C D E F G A B C
T
A
B
8 5 7 8 5 7 4 5

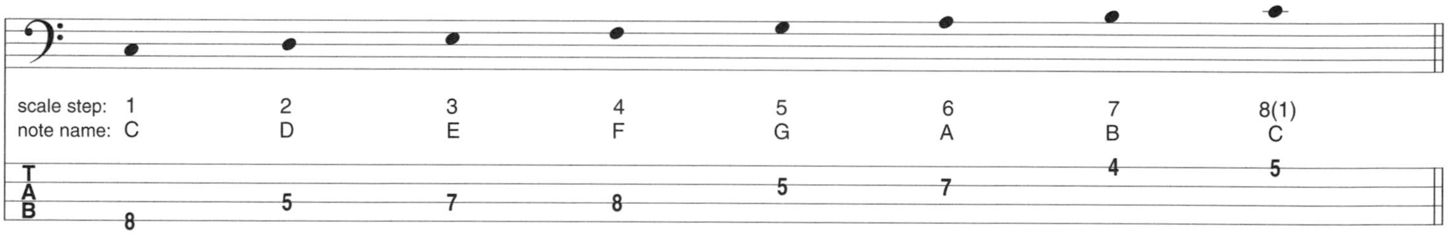

By learning these two patterns well, it is possible to find the correct notes for a major scale in any key, as well as the chords that make up a key center. These patterns are the same for five- and six-string bass.

Building the F Major Scale

We use the same interval formula as before to create the F major scale. In the following diagram, the scale is built on one string. This makes it easy to see where the whole and half steps are located. Shifting a pattern (scale) like this, into a new key center, is known as *transposing.*

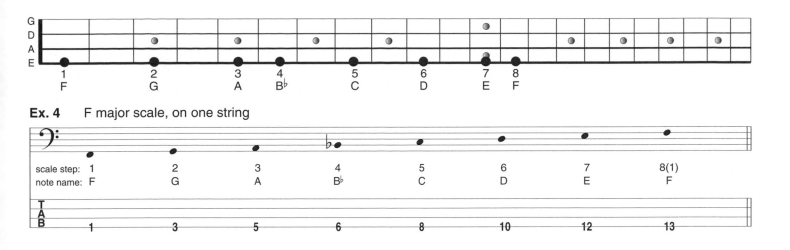

Chapter 2

Ex. 4   F major scale, on one string

scale step:	1	2	3	4	5	6	7	8(1)
note name:	F	G	A	B♭	C	D	E	F

Here is the same scale shown using the second-finger diatonic pattern. However, in this case you will actually begin by playing the root note with your first finger due to the appearance of the open string notes in this particular position. Note the fingering shown.

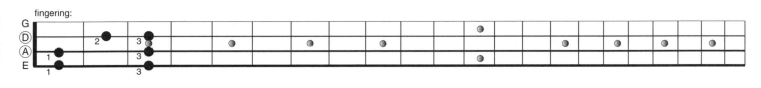

Ex. 5   F major scale, "second-finger" diatonic

scale step:	1	2	3	4	5	6	7	8(1)
note name:	F	G	A	B♭	C	D	E	F

The fourth-finger diatonic pattern below looks the same as that used previously. This F major scale is one octave higher than that shown above.

Ex. 6   F major scale, fourth-finger diatonic

scale step:	1	2	3	4	5	6	7	8(1)
note name:	F	G	A	B♭	C	D	E	F

This last pattern is the same F major scale using second-finger diatonic and starting from the A string.

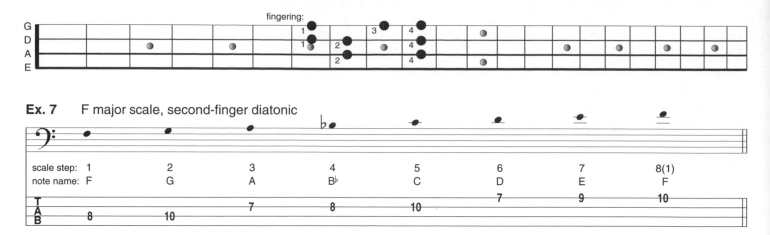

Ex. 7 F major scale, second-finger diatonic

Summary

- **Notes of the major scale:** The major scale is made up of seven different pitches, each with a different letter name given to it.

- **Interval formula:** The quality of any scale, including the major scale, is determined by the arrangement of whole and half steps from the root note. In a major scale, half steps occur between the third and fourth notes of the scale, and between the seventh and eighth notes of the scale. Whole steps occur between all other notes.

- **Transposing:** A major scale may be built upon any starting pitch. Simply make sure that the seven pitches duplicate the proper interval pattern of whole and half steps.

- **Fingering patterns:** The two most common major scale fingering patterns are second-finger diatonic and fourth-finger diatonic. Note: If you play a four-string instrument, learn second-finger diatonic starting on both the E and A strings, and fourth-finger diatonic starting on the E string only. If you play a five- or six-string instrument, learn second-finger diatonic starting on the B, E, and A strings, and fourth-finger diatonic starting on the B and E strings.

3 More Major Scale Fingerings

Background

The major scale can be played in many different ways. Which fingering pattern to use in any given situation is determined by many factors, including style, dramatic effect, ease of playing, and tone. One of the main goals of this book will be to learn the major scale over every area of the neck. This will enable you to relate all areas of the neck to any key and help you link the entire fretboard.

Single-Octave Fingerings

The following diagrams illustrate several methods in which to organize single-octave major scale fingerings—in this case, for G major. There are many more possibilities available, each with its own good and bad points. However, it is not necessary to learn every conceivable option. Each new song you learn will present different fingering problems to solve, and it is best to stay adaptable to new situations. Play through each of the following patterns using the fingering indicated. Optional fingerings are shown in parentheses.

Position Shifts

The first two diagrams below show logical fingering patterns, with one finger per fret and position shifts, which accomodate the major scale on any two adjacent strings. Play each pattern until you have it memorized. The staff and TAB have been omitted; the fretboard patterns should be your main focus.

Ex. 1   G major scale

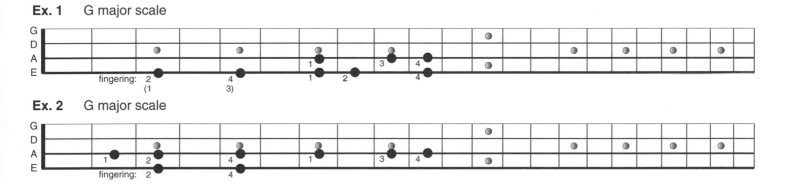

Ex. 2   G major scale

Extended Fingerings

These fingerings are often referred to as "extended fingerings" because they require some extra stretching of the fretting hand.

Ex. 3   G major scale

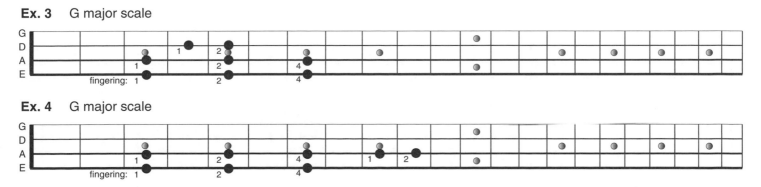

Ex. 4   G major scale

Sliding a Finger

These diagrams illustrate how a major scale can be performed by playing a note and then sliding that finger up or down the neck to play the next note.

Ex. 5   G major scale

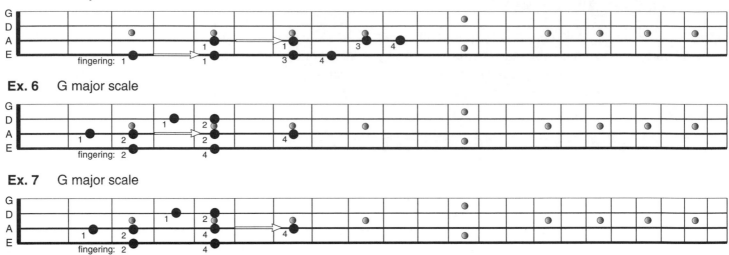

Ex. 6   G major scale

Ex. 7   G major scale

Review

Now we will combine all major scale fingerings covered so far.

Single String: F major scale

Second-Finger Diatonic: C major scale

Fourth-Finger Diatonic: C major scale

Extended-Fingering: G major scales

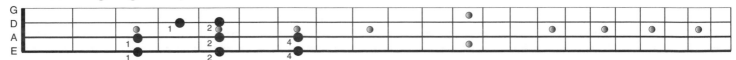

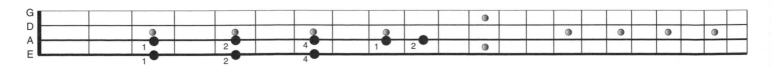

Chapter 3

Shifting: G major scales

Sliding: G major scales

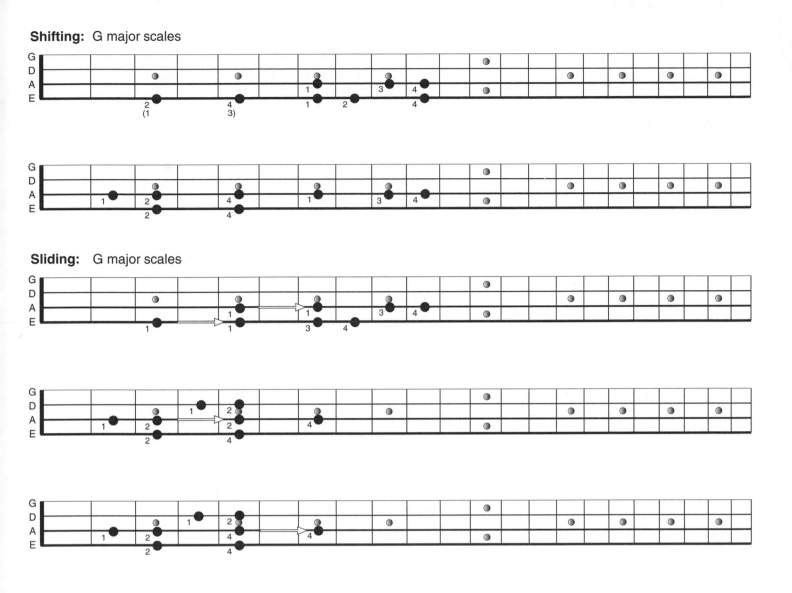

Intervals
4

Background

An *interval* is the distance between two notes. A unique interval name is given to each different distance that notes are spaced apart from one another. We will begin by looking at all the possible intervals up to one octave.

The specific interval names are based on a numbering system that directly reflects the number of letter names spanned by each pair of notes. However, this numbering gives us only a general measurement. To achieve exact precision, we need to know exactly how many half steps lie between the notes. This is accomplished by using modifying terms such as "major," "minor," "perfect," "augmented," or "diminished." For example, "fourth" intervals are always four letter names apart (as we saw in Tuning, page 7) . But there are three different possible types of fourths: "perfect fourths," "augmented fourths," and "diminished fourths." (Perfect fourths were used in Tuning.)

Interval Names

Rather than having to count the number of half steps between each pair of notes, it is easier and quicker to simply memorize the fretboard shapes of each interval to determine its quality.

Each set of diagrams below shows two different ways that interval can appear—first on one string, showing the number of half steps (frets) the notes are apart, and then across strings, which is the more common way of visualizing and playing the interval. We begin with a unison (two notes of the same pitch) and increase the size of each subsequent interval one fret at a time. To emphasize the fact that these shapes may appear anywhere on the neck, we will also vary the starting pitch, or *root.* In particular, memorize the diagrams to the right.

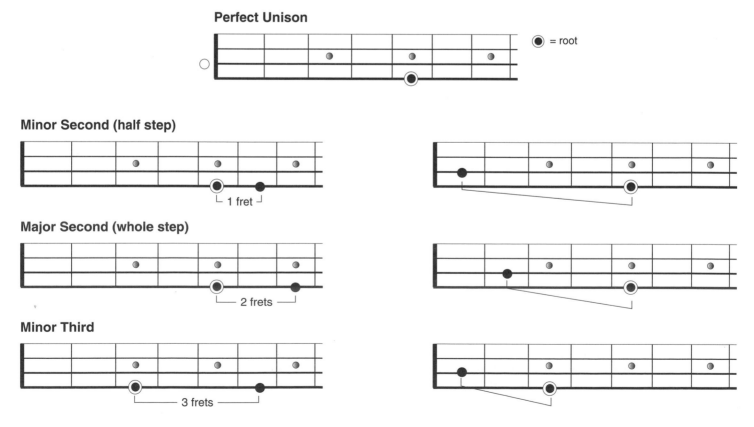

Perfect Unison

● = root

Minor Second (half step)

└ 1 fret ┘

Major Second (whole step)

└── 2 frets ──┘

Minor Third

└── 3 frets ──┘

Chapter 4

Major Third

— 4 frets —

Perfect Fourth

— 5 frets —

Augmented Fourth (or Diminished Fifth)

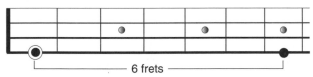

— 6 frets —

Perfect Fifth

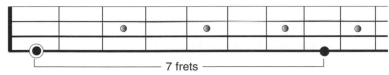

— 7 frets —

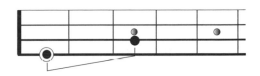

Augmented Fifth (or Minor Sixth)

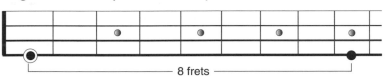

— 8 frets —

Major Sixth

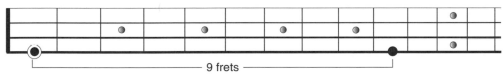

— 9 frets —

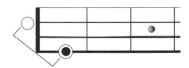

Minor Seventh

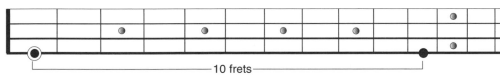

—10 frets—

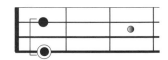

Major Seventh

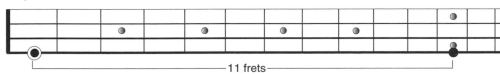

—11 frets—

Perfect Octave

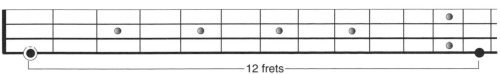

—12 frets—

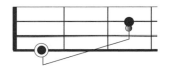

Triads

5

Background

A *triad* is a three-note chord consisting of a root note (which names the triad) and two additional notes located a third interval and a fifth interval above that root note. There are four different types of triads, determined by the different qualities of thirds and fifths.

Types of Triads

Each set of diagrams and examples below illustrates the shape of a particular type of triad, played as an *arpeggio* (one note at a time, in sequence)—as well as the interval formulas and fingerings. As with intervals, these shapes may appear anywhere on the neck.

Major Triad

A major triad is a three-note chord consisting of a root, major third, and perfect fifth.

Ex. 1   G major triads

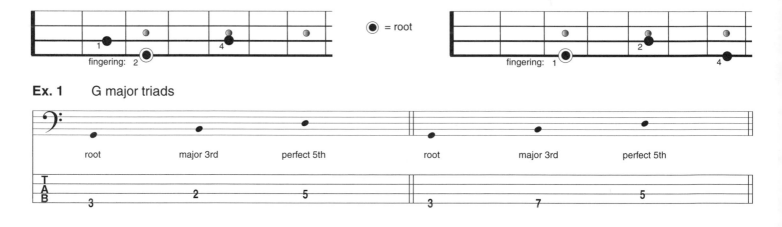

Minor Triad

A minor triad is a three-note chord consisting of a root, minor third, and perfect fifth.

Ex. 2   G minor triads

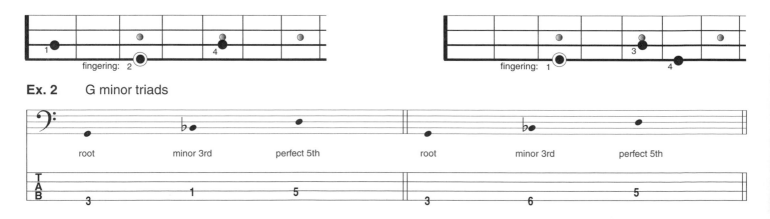

Chapter 5

Diminished Triad

A diminished triad is a three-note chord consisting of a root, minor third, and diminished fifth.

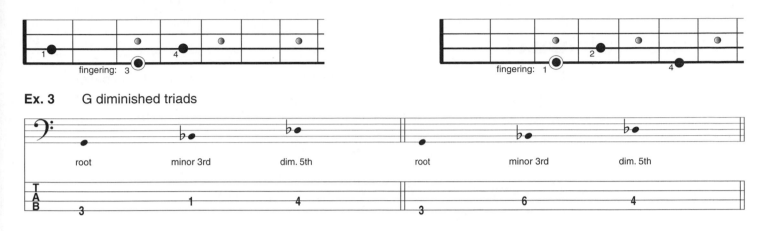

Ex. 3   G diminished triads

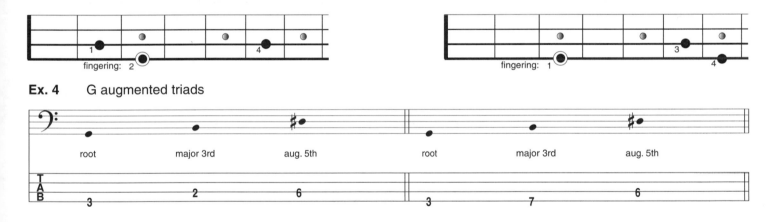

Augmented Triad

An augmented triad is a three-note chord consisting of a root, major third, and augmented fifth.

Ex. 4   G augmented triads

Two-Octave Major Scales 6 and Sequencing

Background

These two-octave scale patterns will help us connect the different regions of the neck and become more familiar with different shifting approaches. The following fingerings for the G major scale offer the most practical approaches for most playing situations. Generally, the scale pattern to use in any particular playing situation is the one containing the most notes used in the song.

G Major Fingerings Beginning on the E String

Play each of the following two-octave G major scale patterns, starting on the E string. The number next to each note specifies the fingering to use.

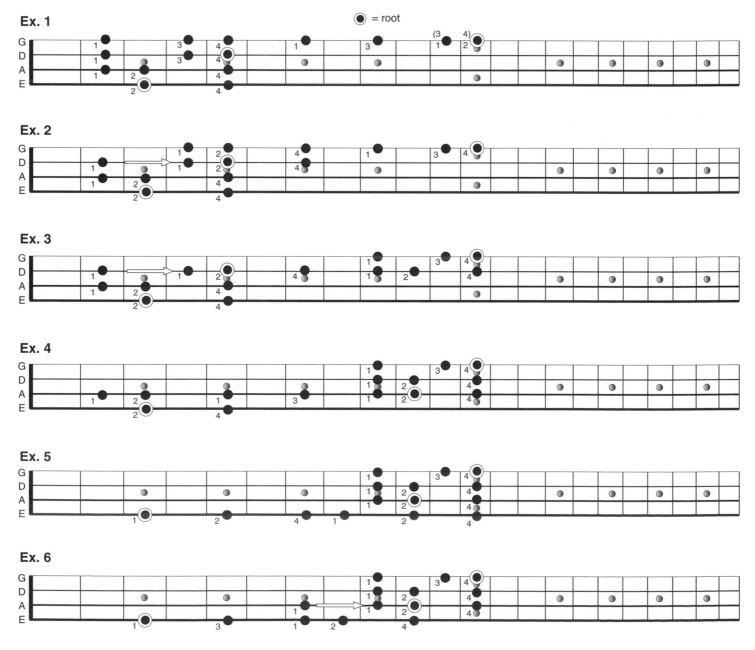

Ex. 7

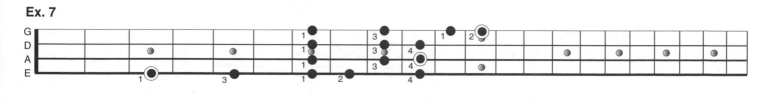

Ex. 8

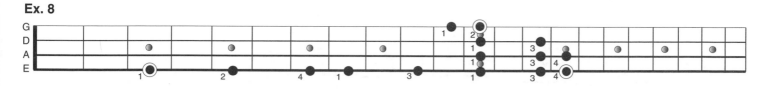

Ex. 9

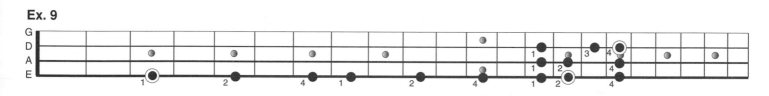

Ex. 10

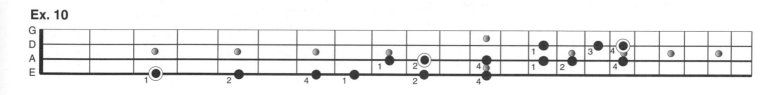

Ex. 11

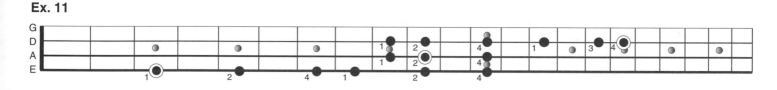

Ex. 12

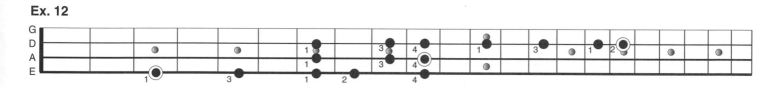

Ex. 13

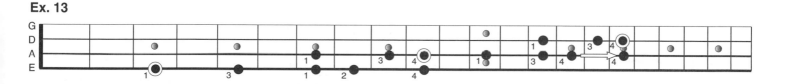

Scale Sequencing

Sequencing is a common melodic device that may be applied to scales, arpeggios, and intervals. Simply put, a *sequence* is a pattern of notes that is repeated at different pitch levels. The following sequences are each applied to the preceeding two-octave G major scale patterns.

The first is a triplet sequence (scale tones: 1–2–3, 2–3–4, etc.). It is applied to the scale pattern shown in Exercise 1, first ascending, then descending. Notice that the fingering must be altered slightly in terms of shifting.

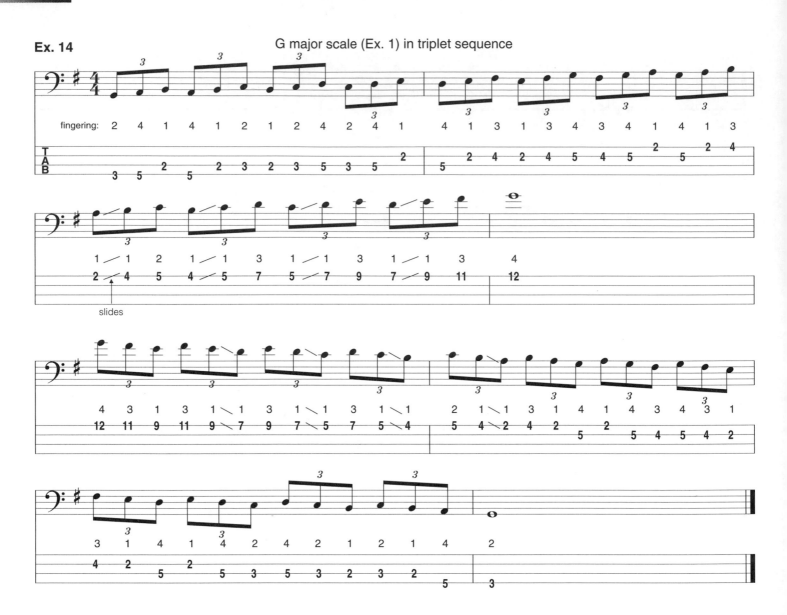

Ex. 14

G major scale (Ex. 1) in triplet sequence

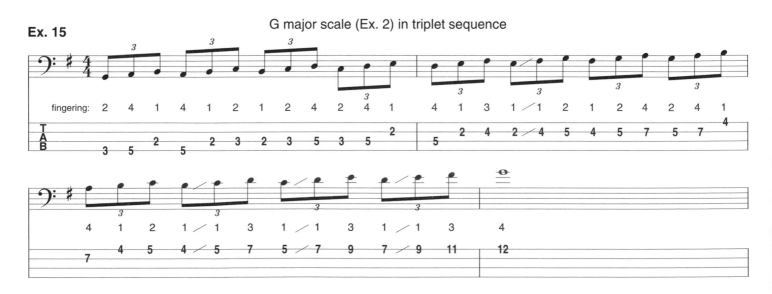

Below, the triplet sequence is applied to the scale pattern from Exercise 2. When finished with this example, continue by applying the same triplet sequence to the remaining G major fingering patterns (Exercises 1-13).

Ex. 15

G major scale (Ex. 2) in triplet sequence

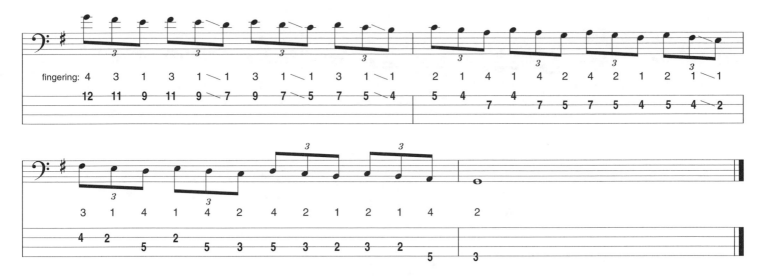

The next sequence is in groups of four notes (scale tones: 1–2–3–4, 2–3–4–5, etc.). Below, it is applied to the G major scale pattern shown in Exercise 3, but continue by applying this sequence to each of the patterns previously shown.

G major scale (Ex. 3) in basic four-note sequence

Ex. 16

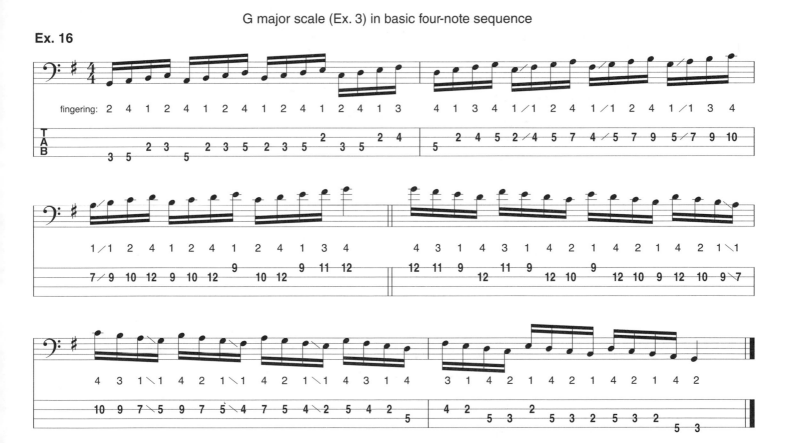

The third, fourth, fifth, and sixth sequences are also in groups of four but contain interval skips. Below they are applied to the G major scale pattern shown in Exercise 4, but continue by applying these sequences to each of the patterns. Note: These exercises are shown here ascending only, but you may invert the patterns and practice the descending portions as well.

G major scale (Ex. 4) in various four-note sequences

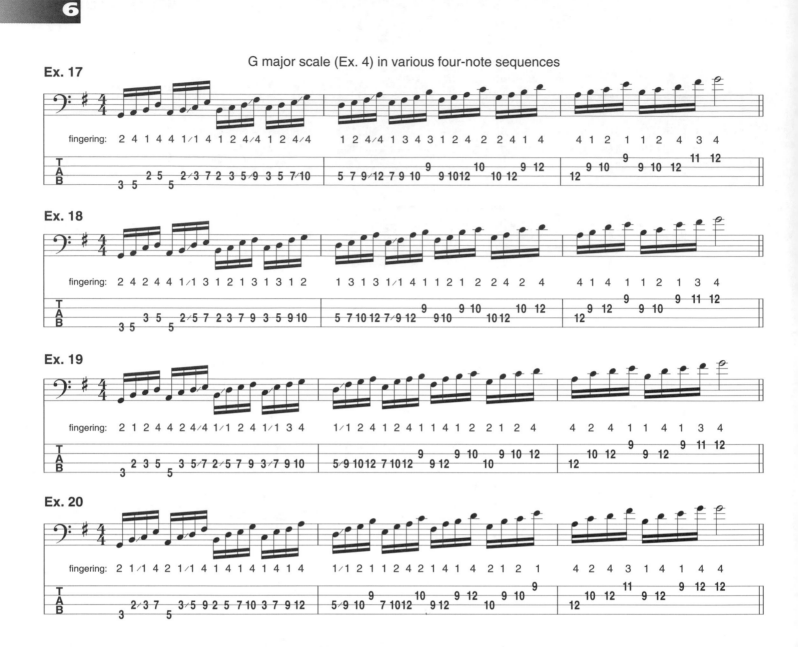

The following two sequences incorporate triad shapes. Here, the sequence is applied to the G major pattern shown in Exercise 5, but continue by applying each of these sequences to each of the patterns.

G major scale (Ex. 15) with triadic sequences

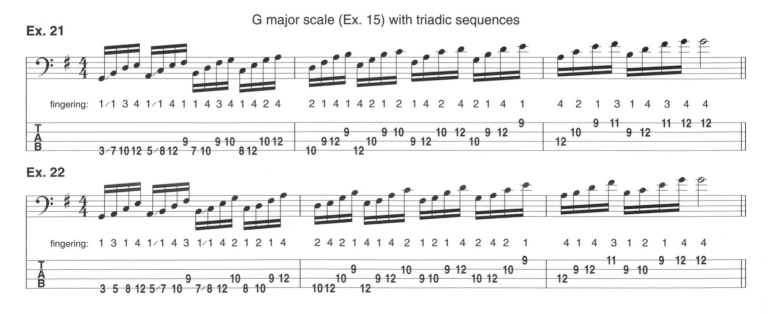

The next three sequences show still more variations to practice. They are applied to the patterns of Exercises 6 and 7, but continue by applying each of these sequences to each of the patterns.

G major scale (Ex. 6) with more sequences in groups of four

Ex. 23

Ex. 24

G major scale (Ex. 7) with pedal tone in sequence of four

Ex. 25

The next three sequences reverse the motif pattern and start on the third note (B) of the scale. They are applied to Exerclsese 8-10, but continue by applying each of these sequences to each of the patterns.

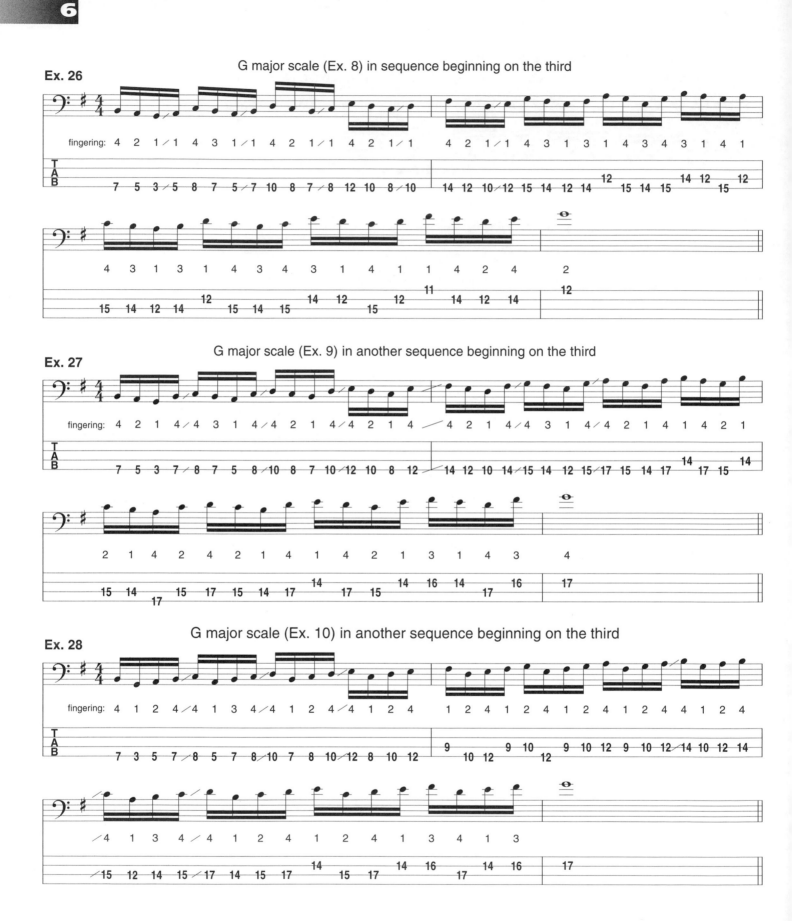

Ex. 26

G major scale (Ex. 8) in sequence beginning on the third

Ex. 27

G major scale (Ex. 9) in another sequence beginning on the third

Ex. 28

G major scale (Ex. 10) in another sequence beginning on the third

The last four sequences use two-note interval-skipping patterns. They are applied to the major scale patterns of Exercises 11-13, but continue by applying each of these sequences to each of the patterns on pages 20-21.

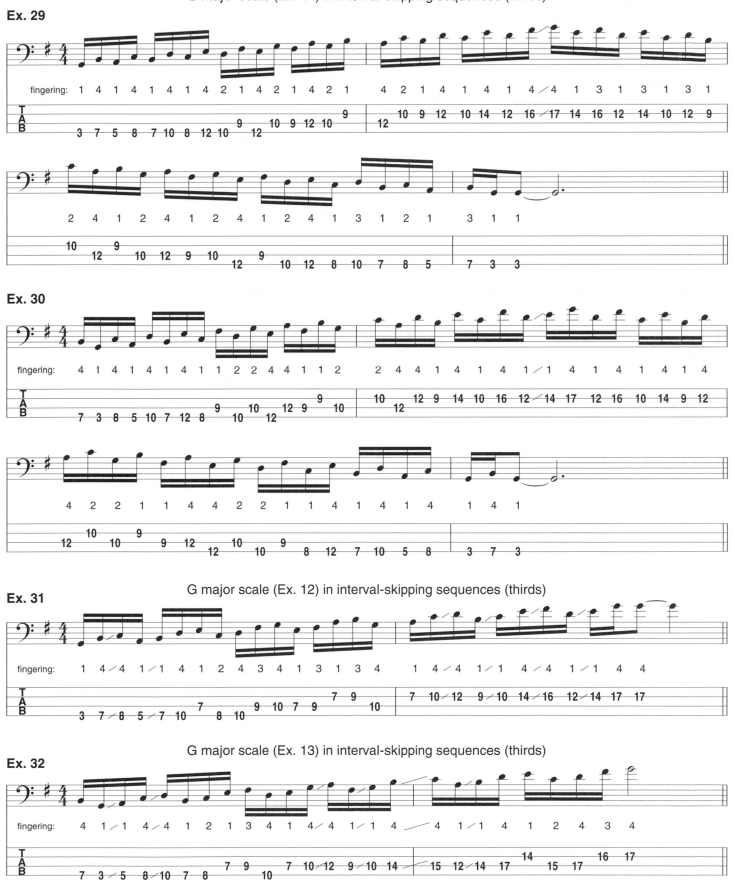

Extended Two-Octave Fingerings

Background

The following two-octave major scales show extended fingerings beginning from the E string, as well as from the A and D strings. This will tend to require even more movement up and down the fretboard. Emphasize smooth shifting and try to eliminate any gaps between notes.

More Two-Octave Fingerings

Extended Fingerings

The following two-octave G major scale patterns use the extended or "stretched" scale shape with some shifting. Play up and down each pattern using the fingering shown.

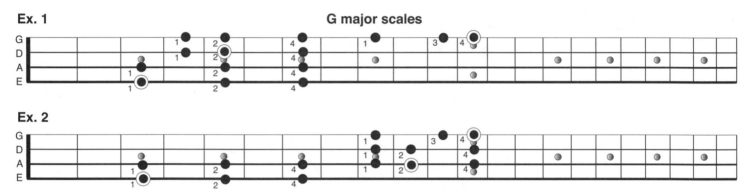

Beginning on the A String

The following two-octave C major scale patterns begin on the A string. Play up and down each with the fingering shown.

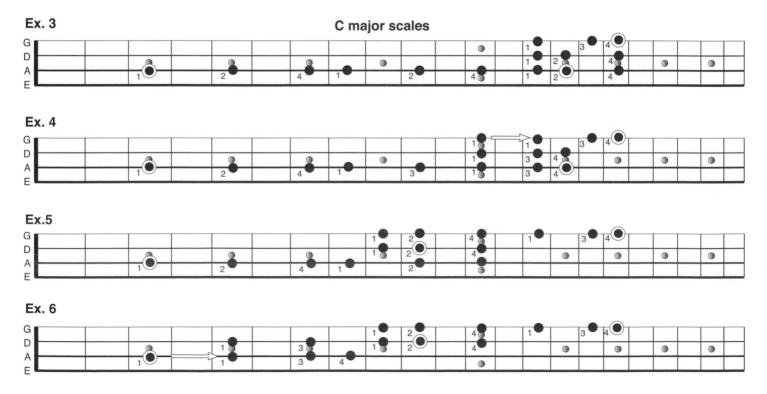

26

Chapter 7

Beginning on the D String

These two-octave E♭ major scale patterns begin on the D string. Play up and down each with the fingering shown.

Ex. 7   E♭ major scales

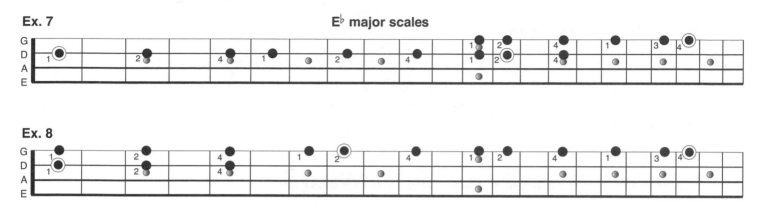

Ex. 8

Now, apply the previous chapter's scale sequence patterns to the fingerings shown in this chapter as well.

Summary

- Two-octave major scale fingerings provide access to higher regions of the neck and help organize the neck into diatonic structures.

- Extra care should be taken to eliminate the gap between notes when shifting between positions.

- The application of scale sequences to the two-octave fingerings creates greater melodic interest than simply playing the scales in stepwise order.

Modal Patterns

8

Background

Modal patterns are one-octave scale shapes derived from the diatonic major scale. Each modal pattern starts on a different note of the major scale, giving us a total of seven different modal shapes (from the seven notes of the major scale). The modal names are *Ionian, Dorian, Phrygian, Lydian, Mixolydian, Aeolian,* and *Locrian.*

Modal Patterns in G Major

The following diagram illustrates all the notes on the neck (no open strings) that make up the key of G major.

Since this is too much information to memorize effectively, we can break up the major scale into a number of one-octave segments. This makes learning the pattern easier and solves other problems as well. Each one-octave segment starts from a different note of the major scale, and comprises a separate fingering. These are commonly referred to as *modal patterns.*

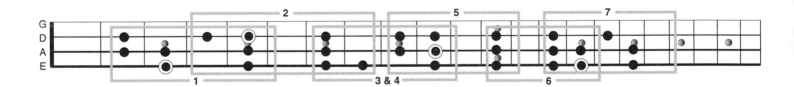

Modal patterns offer several advantages:

- A seamless connection of higher and lower diatonic scale patterns.

- The proper mode and related fingering for each diatonic chord in a key.

- Coverage of intermediate areas of the neck, which facilitates better sight reading.

Exercise 1 illustrates each pattern separately, with the accompanying modal names. Play each pattern and memorize its shape.

Chapter 8

Ex. 1

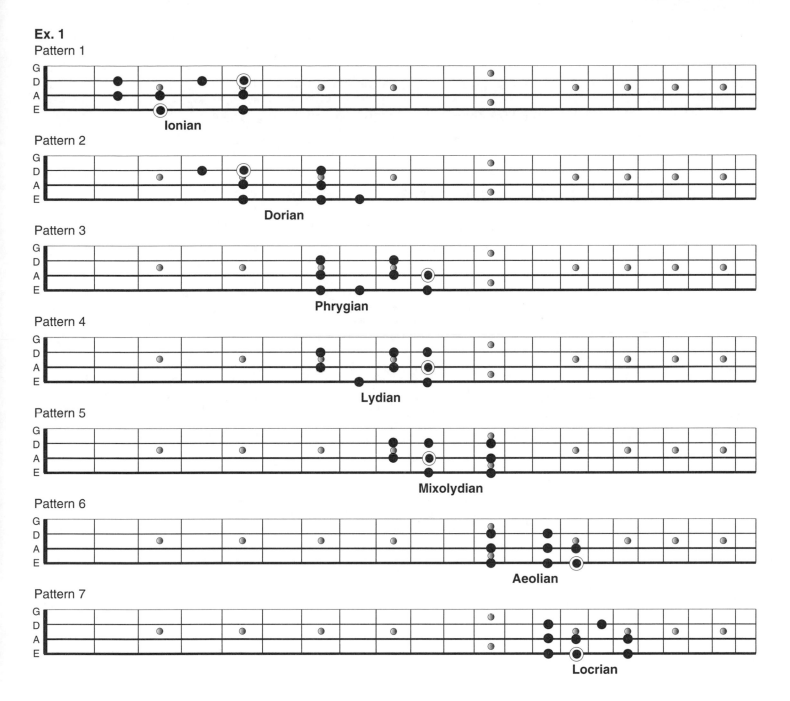

Analyzing the Modes

The following table lays out several specific aspects of the modes, including the pattern number as used above, the starting note relative to the steps of the major scale, and the location of all half steps within that mode.

Mode name:	Pattern #:	Begins on:	Half steps:
Ionian	pattern 1	major scale step 1	3–4 and 7–8
Dorian	pattern 2	major scale step 2	2–3 and 6–7
Phrygian	pattern 3	major scale step 3	1–2 and 5–6
Lydian	pattern 4	major scale step 4	4–5 and 7–8
Mixolydian	pattern 5	major scale step 5	3–4 and 6–7
Aeolian	pattern 6	major scale step 6	2–3 and 5–6
Locrian	pattern 7	major scale step 7	1–2 and 4–5

The modal patterns can also be broken down into their respective sounds much like chord types.

> **Major-sounding modes:** Ionian, Lydian, Mixolydian
>
> **Minor-sounding modes:** Dorian, Phrygian, Aeolian
>
> **Diminished-sounding mode:** Locrian

Modal Patterns in C Major

The set of diagrams below illustrates the same system of modal patterns applied in the key of C major. Notice that the patterns are the same as before.

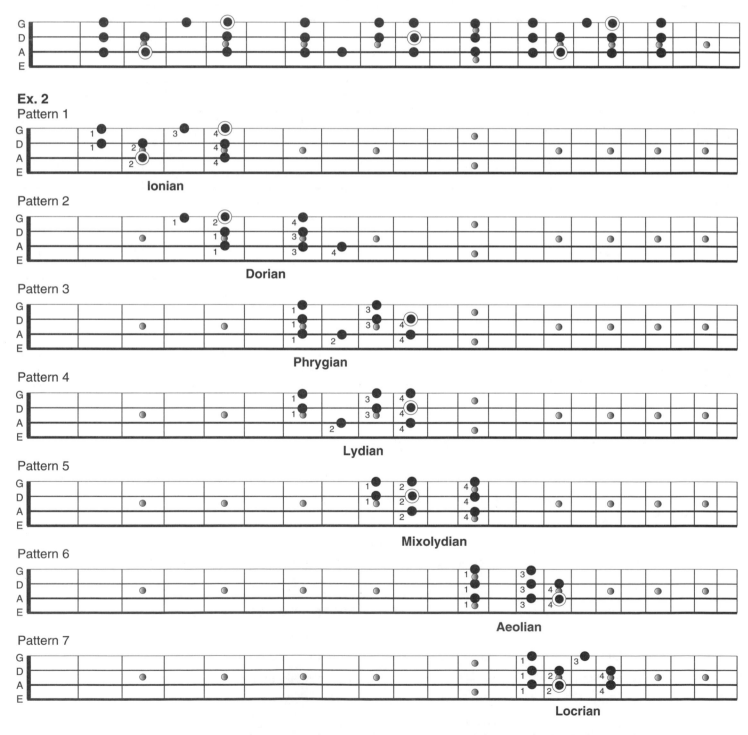

Notes on higher or lower strings can be added to each of the patterns when needed.

More Major Keys

9

Background

In this chapter, we will encounter major key centers that lie on the fretboard in such a way that modal patterns appear both above and below pattern 1 (unlike in the previous chapter, where pattern 1 was always the lowest pattern).

A♭ Major

The following diagrams show the modal patterns in A♭ major. Remember, notes can be added above or below a pattern to fill out a position. It is also helpful to remember where the half steps occur in each mode. Note: Patterns 1 and 7 are virtually the same pattern since they occur in the same position. This is also true of patterns 3 and 4.

Play through and memorize the modal patterns in the key of A♭.

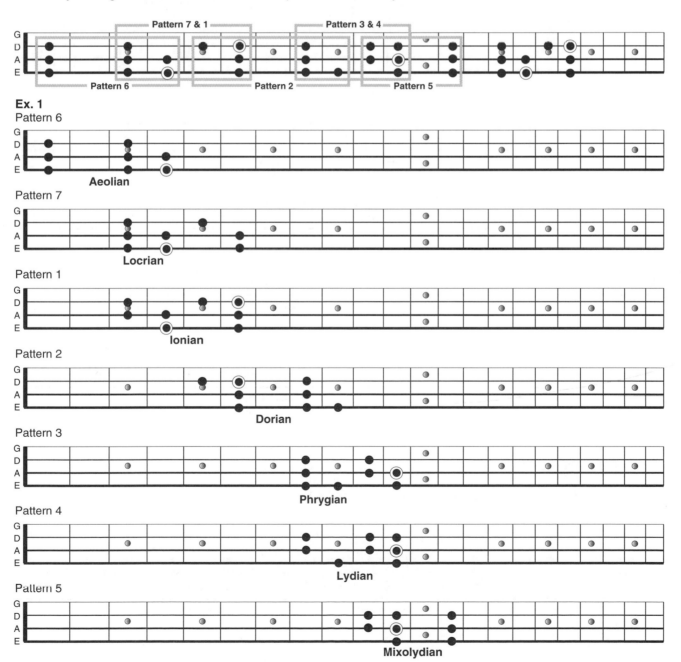

D♭ Major

The diagrams below illustrate the modal patterns in D♭ major.

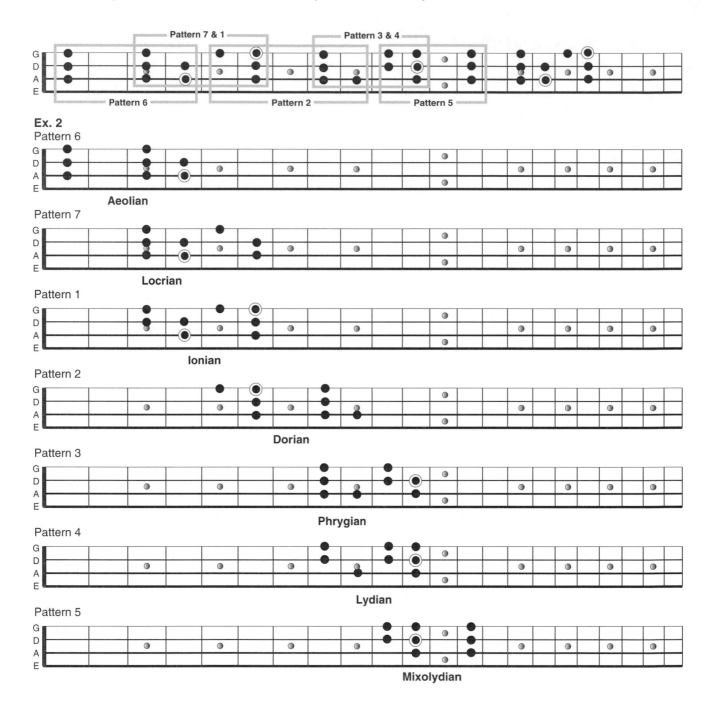

Ex. 2

Pattern 6 — Aeolian

Pattern 7 — Locrian

Pattern 1 — Ionian

Pattern 2 — Dorian

Pattern 3 — Phrygian

Pattern 4 — Lydian

Pattern 5 — Mixolydian

E♭ Major

The diagrams below illustrate the modal patterns in E♭ major.

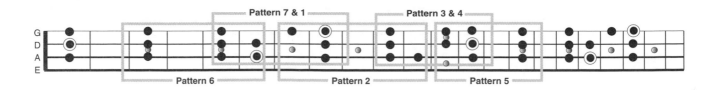

Chapter 9

Ex. 3

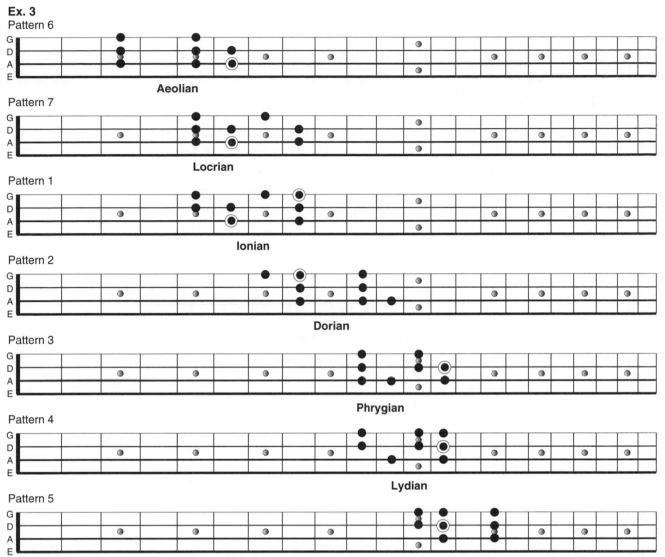

Pattern 6

Aeolian

Pattern 7

Locrian

Pattern 1

Ionian

Pattern 2

Dorian

Pattern 3

Phrygian

Pattern 4

Lydian

Pattern 5

Mixolydian

10 Other Common Scale Types

Background

The *natural minor* scale plays the same relative role in music written in a minor key as the major scale plays in music written in a major key. The natural minor scale (or Aeolian mode) and its related scale harmony lie at the heart of virtually any song in a minor key.

Pentatonic scales are also quite important. They are among the most common scales for creating bass lines, solos, and fills, and they form the basis for many popular music styles such as rhythm 'n' blues, gospel, rock, country and western, and others. Pentatonic scales also provide a palette of colorful sounds for fusion and jazz.

Fingerings for A Natural Minor

The following diagrams and example show the two most efficient single-octave fingerings for the natural minor scale.

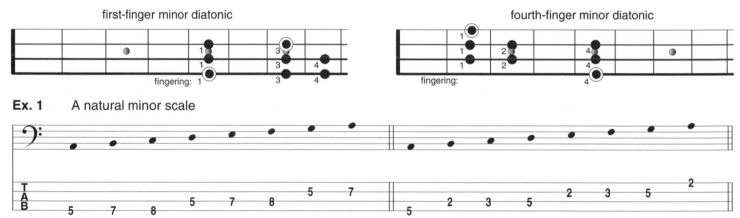

Ex. 1   A natural minor scale

Fingerings for A Major Pentatonic

The major pentatonic scale is common to many cultures globally and has as many uses as the cultures that play it. It can be thought of as an "all-purpose" scale for much of popular music. It has also been a great source of material for jazz artists such as McCoy Tyner, Stanley Clarke, and John McLaughlin, to name just a few. The two most efficient fingerings for the major pentatonic scale are shown below.

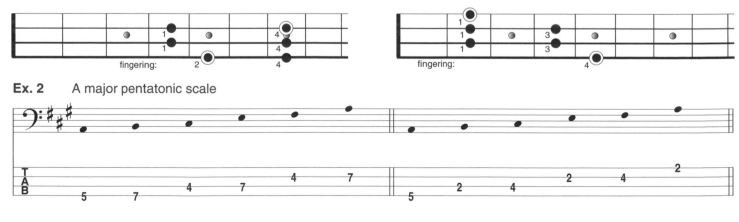

Ex. 2   A major pentatonic scale

Fingerings for G Minor Pentatonic

The minor pentatonic scale works with minor chords in the same way that the major pentatonic works with major chords. It is quite common in rock and blues music. The diagrams below illustrate the most common fingerings.

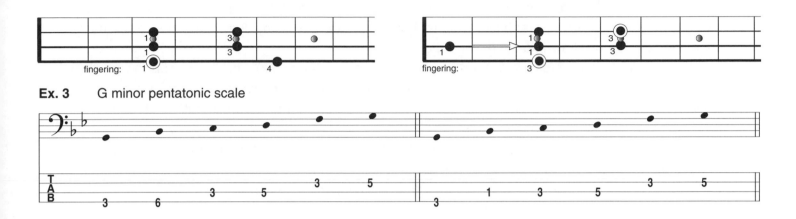

Ex. 3   G minor pentatonic scale

11 The Harmonized Major Scale

Background

A *key center* specifies the central pitch of a song. It is supported by chords that keep the ear focused around that one central pitch, or *tonic*. For songs in a major key, the notes making up these supporting chords are drawn from a major scale.

Specifically, these chords are derived from a major scale by *harmonizing* the scale. This means that chords are built upon each note of the scale by stacking up third intervals—utilizing notes drawn exclusively from that scale—until triads are formed. The resulting set of seven chords is referred to as the "scale harmony" or the "diatonic triads" of a key.

In contemporary styles (rock, fusion, pop, and jazz), other chords exist that do not fit into this system, but which are combined with the diatonic triads to reinforce the tonal center. Still, in most cases, the majority of the chords in a song will be taken from the harmonized scale.

Harmonizing the G Major Scale

Below, the G major scale is laid out on one string, then harmonized in thirds, and finally in triads. The neck diagrams will help you better visualize this process of harmonization.

Ex. 1   G major scale

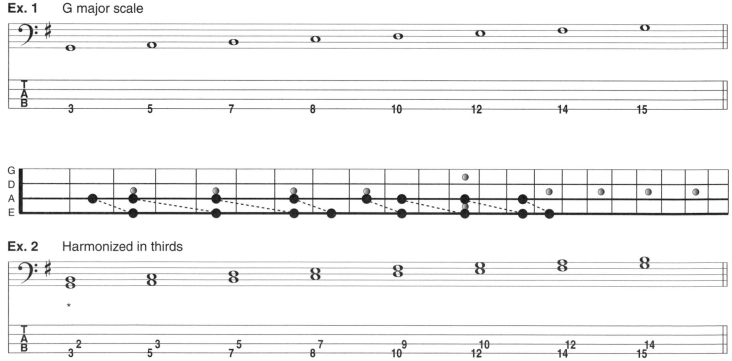

Ex. 2   Harmonized in thirds

*Play notes one after another, let ring together.

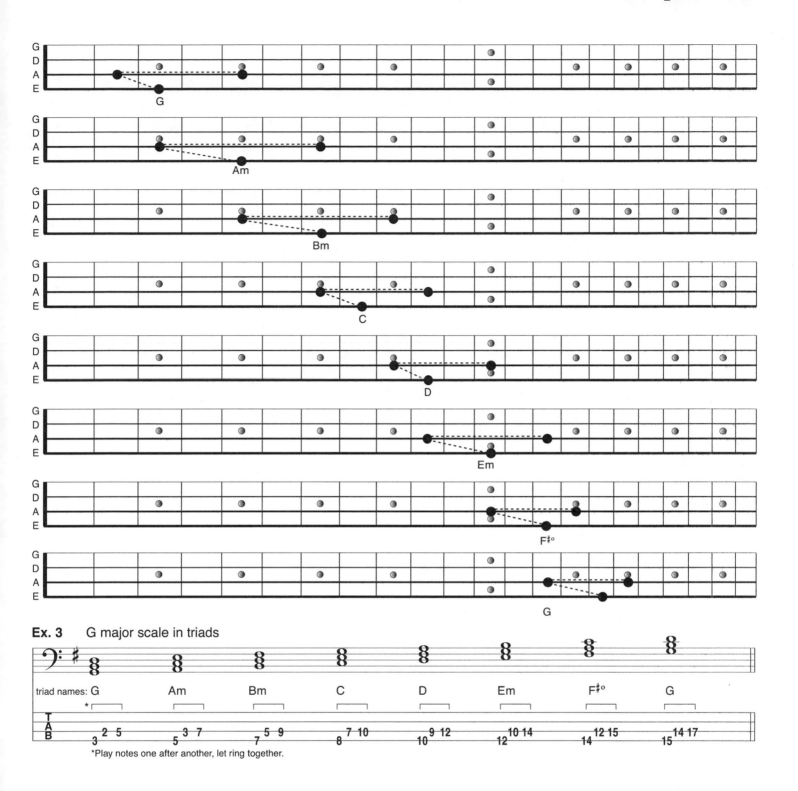

Ex. 3 G major scale in triads

triad names: G   Am   Bm   C   D   Em   F#°   G

*Play notes one after another, let ring together.

Roman numerals are commonly used to indicate each chord's function relative to the tonic. Upper-case Roman numerals indicate that the chord has a major third (i.e., is a major chord), while lower-case Roman numerals indicate that the chord has a minor third (i.e., is a minor or diminished chord). Below, the triads are labeled using this Roman numeral system.

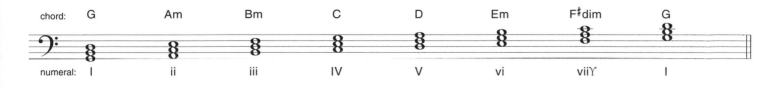

chord: G   Am   Bm   C   D   Em   F#dim   G

numeral: I   ii   iii   IV   V   vi   viiϒ   I

It is also possible to play the harmonized scale moving *across* the strings in one position, rather than moving up the neck. Exercise 4 shows the arpeggios of the triads in G major, beginning with the second-finger diatonic position. Exercise 5 shows the arpeggios of the triads in G major, beginning with the fourth-finger diatonic position at the fifteenth fret.

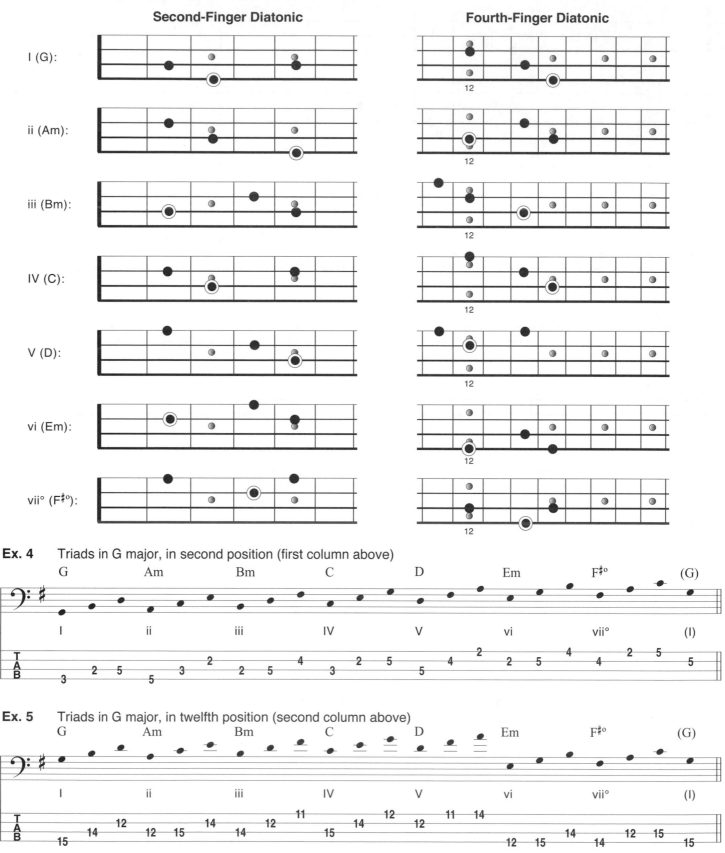

Second-Finger Diatonic

Fourth-Finger Diatonic

I (G):

ii (Am):

iii (Bm):

IV (C):

V (D):

vi (Em):

vii° (F#°):

Ex. 4 Triads in G major, in second position (first column above)

Ex. 5 Triads in G major, in twelfth position (second column above)

The quality and sequence of the chords in any harmonized major scale remains the same for all major keys.

Analysis

After you learn the major scale harmony, it is then possible to know what scales (or modes) can be used to play a song by simply looking at the chords used. For Exercise 6, analyze the function (Roman numeral) of each chord and write it in the space provided. Also, write in the pattern number associated with that chord. The correct answers are given at the bottom of the page.

Ex. 6

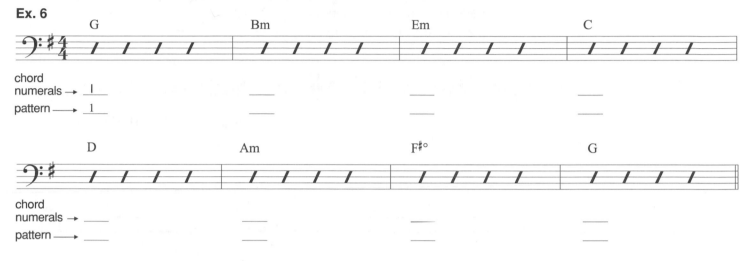

chord
numerals → I ___   ___   ___   ___

pattern → 1 ___   ___   ___   ___

chord
numerals → ___   ___   ___   ___

pattern → ___   ___   ___   ___

Summary

- Major scales can be harmonized in thirds to obtain the scale harmony for the key center.

- It is very important to memorize the scale harmony for all major keys.

- Being able to analyze the chords of a progression yields important information about a song, such as the key center, available notes, and the possible scale patterns that can be used.

Answers:

Exercise 6:   Bm=iii, pattern 3; Em=vi, pattern 6; C=IV, pattern 4; D=V, pattern 5; Am=ii, pattern 2; F♯°=vii°, pattern 7; G=I, pattern 1.

The Harmonized
12 Minor Scale

Background

The process of learning the scale harmony for the minor keys is much the same as with the major keys. We begin with a natural minor scale and stack up third intervals to create triads.

Harmonizing the A Natural Minor Scale

The diagrams and staves below illustrate the harmonization process for A minor. The final staff system shows the Roman numeral analysis.

Ex. 1   A natural minor

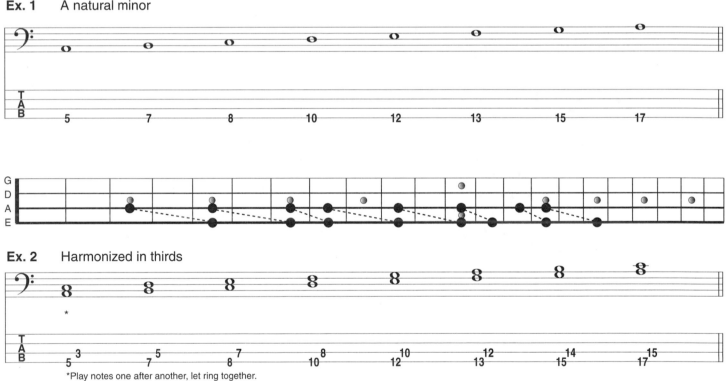

Ex. 2   Harmonized in thirds

*Play notes one after another, let ring together.

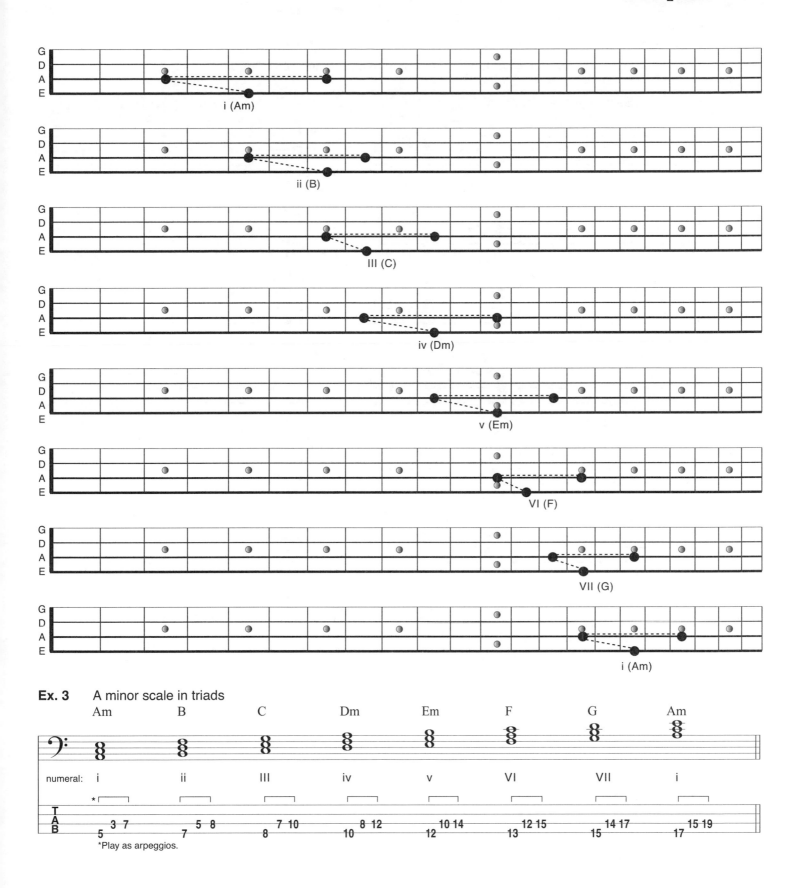

Ex. 3   A minor scale in triads

*Play as arpeggios.

Exercises 4 and 5 show the harmonized A natural minor scale moving across the neck in first-finger diatonic and fourth-finger diatonic positioning, rather than up the neck as before.

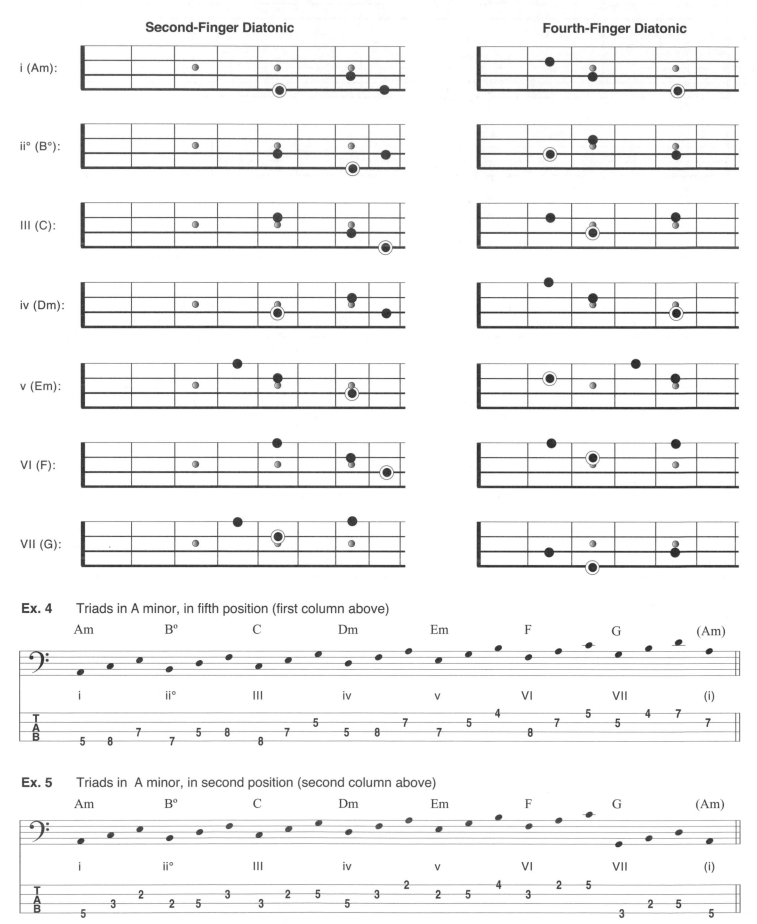

Ex. 4   Triads in A minor, in fifth position (first column above)

Ex. 5   Triads in A minor, in second position (second column above)

Comparing Diatonic Major and Minor Keys

The following table compares the chord qualities of the harmonized diatonic major scale to that of the harmonized diatonic minor scale. In other words, it shows the chord types and their relative positions in both major and minor keys.

Major Key Chords:	Minor Key Chords:
Major types: I–IV–V	Minor types: i–iv–v
Minor types: ii–iii–vi	Major types: III–VI–VII
Diminished: vii°	Diminished: ii°

Analysis

Analyze the following minor key progressions as before, labeling each chord with its appropriate Roman numeral. The answers are given below.

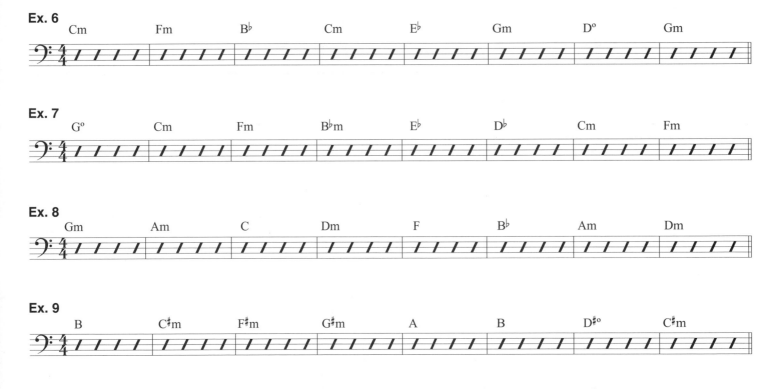

Answers:

Exercise 6:	*Cm=i, Fm=iv, B♭=VII, Cm=i, E♭=III, Gm=v, D°=ii°, Gm=v*
Exercise 7:	*G°=ii°, Cm=v, Fm=i, B♭m=iv, E♭=VII, D♭=VI, Cm=v, Fm=i*
Exercise 8:	*Gm=iv, Am=v, C=VII, Dm=i, F=III, B♭=VI, Am=v, Dm=i*
Exercise 9:	*B=VII, C♯m=i, F♯m=iv, G♯m=v, A=VI, B=VII, D♯°=ii°, C♯m=i*

13 The Harmonized Major Scale in Sevenths

Background

When we add another third interval on top of each triad in the harmonized scale, we extend each chord to become a type of *seventh chord*. Harmonizing the major scale in sevenths reveals some important distinctions as compared to harmonizing the scale only in triads. Specifically, the V chord becomes a *dominant seventh chord*, and it plays a very significant role in progressions. Another important difference is that the vii° chord is extended to become a *minor seven flat five chord*. (The m7♭5 should not be confused with the fully diminished seventh chord, which has a double-flatted seventh.)

Harmonizing G Major into Seventh Chords

The diagrams below illustrate the modal patterns of the G major scale along with the arpeggiated seventh chords in the key of G major. Play through Exercise 1 and memorize both the sequence of seventh chords and their shapes. Notice how each chord arpeggio skips every other note to create third intervals.

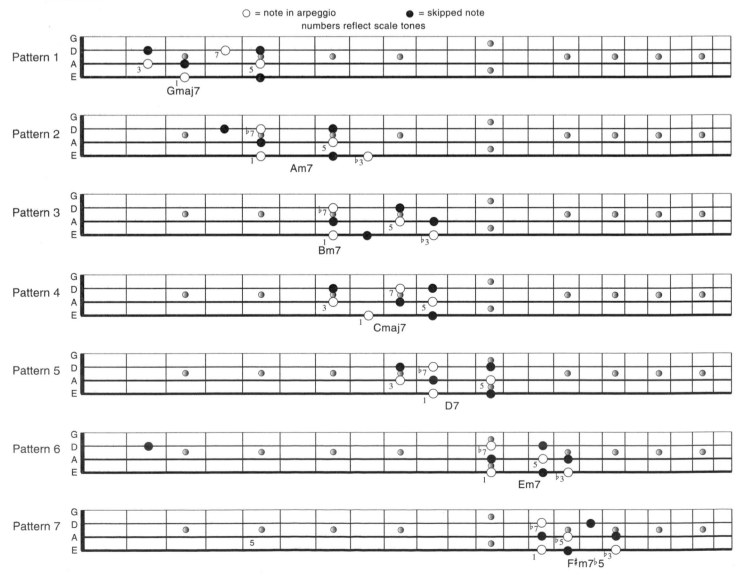

Ex. 1 G major scale, harmonized in seventh chords

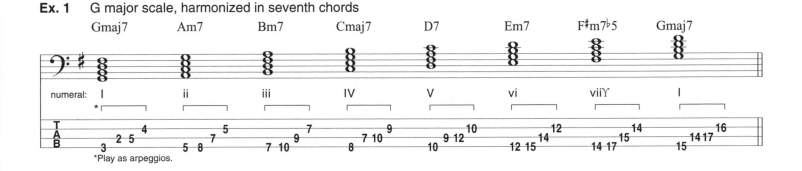

*Play as arpeggios.

Inversions

To play all the diatonic seventh chords across the neck in one position, it will be necessary to invert some of the chord shapes. The following staff demonstrates the process of inverting a G7 chord, and names the specific inversions.

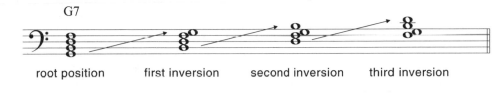

root position   first inversion   second inversion   third inversion

> If the root is the lowest note, the chord is in *root position*.
>
> If the third is the lowest note, the chord is in *first inversion*.
>
> If the fifth is the lowest note, the chord is in *second inversion*.
>
> If the seventh is the lowest note, the chord is in *third linversion*.

Exercise 2 demonstrates playing the diatonic seventh chord arpeggios across the neck beginning with the second-finger diatonic position. Notice that inversions are used, as necessary.

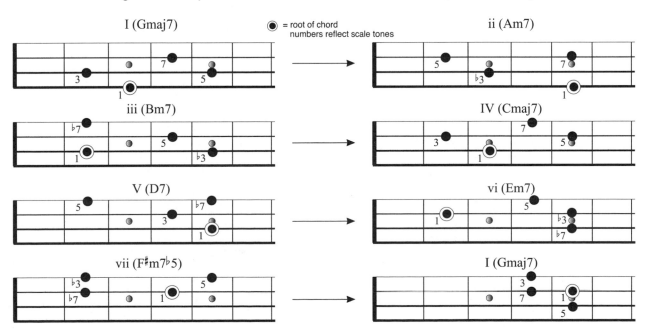

Ex. 2 G major, harmonized in seventh chords, across the neck

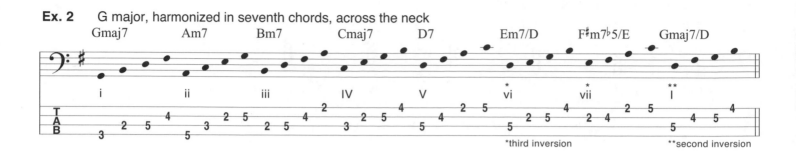

Gmaj7 Am7 Bm7 Cmaj7 D7 Em7/D F#m7♭5/E Gmaj7/D

*third inversion **second inversion

Exercise 3 demonstrates playing the diatonic seventh chord arpeggios across the neck beginning with the fourth-finger diatonic position. Again, notice the inversions used. It is important to learn not only the locations of the chord tones when they appear above the root, but also when they appear below the root.

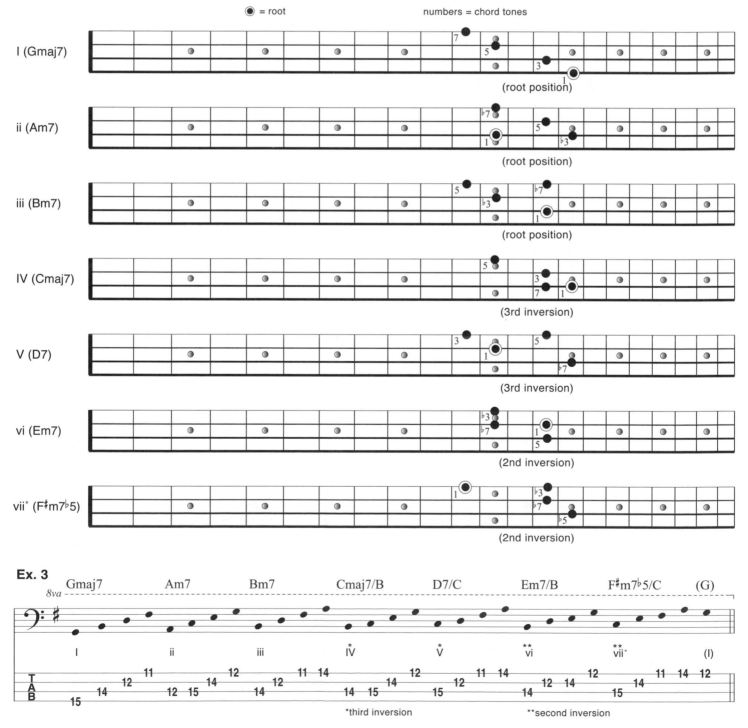

Ex. 3

Gmaj7 Am7 Bm7 Cmaj7/B D7/C Em7/B F#m7♭5/C (G)

I ii iii *IV *V **vi **vii° (I)

*third inversion **second inversion

The Harmonized Minor 14 Scale in Sevenths

Background

Harmonizing the minor scale into seventh chords extends the chord harmonies in a similar way as it does with the major scale, in the previous chapter. The most significant difference is the change of function of the VI chord, which belonged to the tonic family in a major key (shares notes in common with the I chord), but which in a minor key belongs to the subdominant family (shares notes in common with the iv chord).

It is important to memorize the minor scale harmony because in modern songwriting there is a great deal of borrowing chords from the major scale and the *parallel* minor scale. (The parallel minor is a minor scale beginning on the same tonal center.) This idea of combining chords from both major key and minor key centers is referred to as "modal interchange."

Harmonizing G Minor into Seventh Chords

The diagrams below illustrate the modal patterns of the G minor scale along with the arpeggiated seventh chords in that key. Play through Exercise 1 and memorize both the sequence of seventh chords and their shapes. Notice how each chord arpeggio skips every other note to create third intervals.

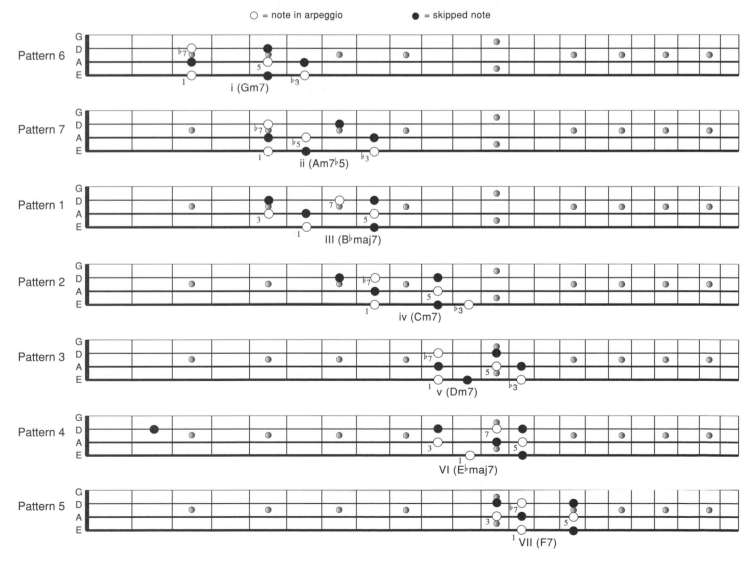

Ex. 1 G natural minor scale, harmonized in seventh chords

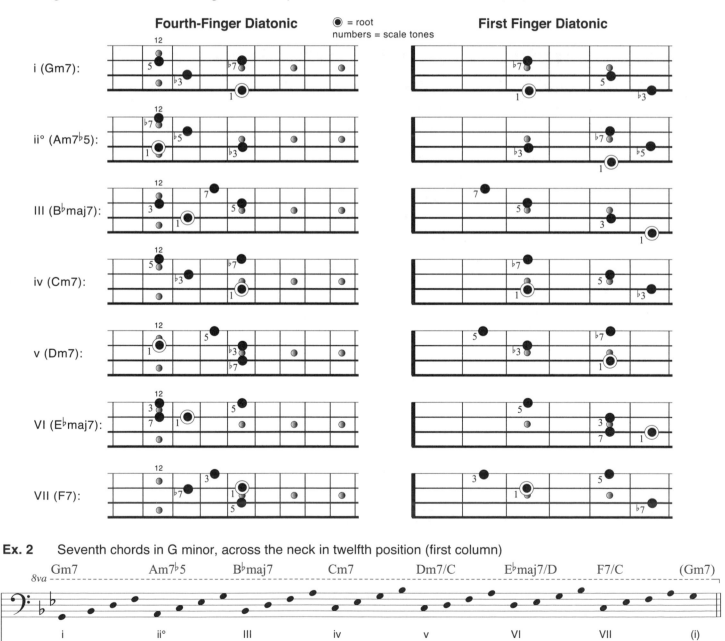

Gm7	Am7♭5	B♭maj7	Cm7	Dm7	E♭maj7	F7	Gm7

** pattern 6   pattern 7   pattern 1   pattern 2   pattern 3   pattern 4   pattern 5   pattern 6
i   ii°   III   iv   v   VI   VII   i

*Play as arpeggios.

** Note how the fingering patterns (modes) align themselves with the minor key chords.

The examples below illustrate the minor diatonic seventh chord arpeggios beginning in both first-finger diatonic and fourth-finger diatonic positions. Inversions are used on v, VI, and VII.

Fourth-Finger Diatonic   ◉ = root   numbers = scale tones   **First Finger Diatonic**

i (Gm7):

ii° (Am7♭5):

III (B♭maj7):

iv (Cm7):

v (Dm7):

VI (E♭maj7):

VII (F7):

Ex. 2 Seventh chords in G minor, across the neck in twelfth position (first column)

Gm7	Am7♭5	B♭maj7	Cm7	Dm7/C	E♭maj7/D	F7/C	(Gm7)
i	ii°	III	iv	v	VI	VII	(i)

Chapter 14

Ex. 3 Seventh chords in G minor, across the neck in third position (second column)

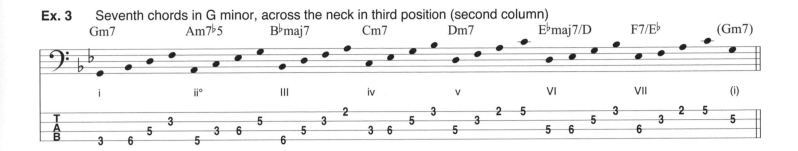

Analysis

Usually, music in a minor key contains a V7 chord that is a dominant-seventh type, as opposed to the naturally occuring minor seventh, because songwriters in most cases prefer the strength of the dominant seventh resolving to the tonic.

Analyze the minor key progressions below. Write out the function (Roman numeral) of each chord and its accompanying modal pattern. Note that the V7 chord may appear as either a dominant-seventh type (V7) or a minor-seventh type (v7).

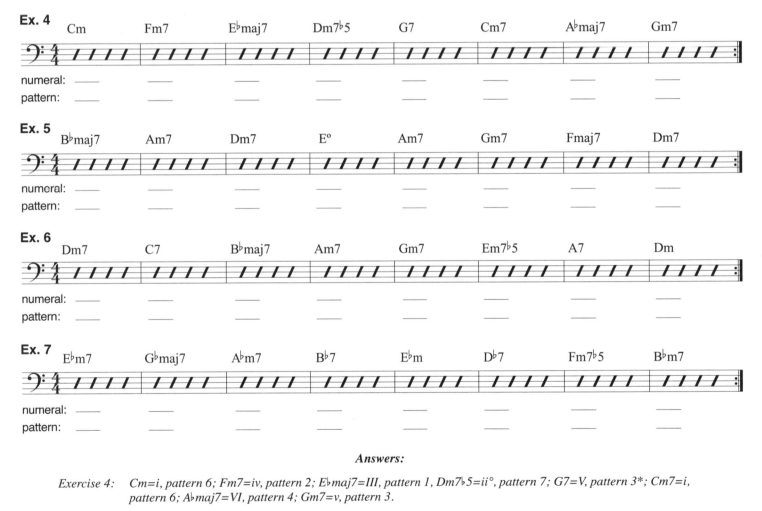

Answers:

Exercise 4: Cm=i, pattern 6; Fm7=iv, pattern 2; E♭maj7=III, pattern 1, Dm7♭5=ii°, pattern 7; G7=V, pattern 3*; Cm7=i, pattern 6; A♭maj7=VI, pattern 4; Gm7=v, pattern 3.

Exercise 5: B♭maj7=VI, pattern 4; Am7=v, pattern 3; Dm7=i, pattern 6; E°=ii°, pattern 7; Am7=v, pattern 3; Gm7=iv, pattern 2; Fmaj7=III, pattern 1; Dm7=i, pattern 6.

Exercise 6: Dm7=i, pattern 6; C7=VII, pattern 5; B♭maj7=VI, pattern 4; Am7=v, pattern 3; Gm7=iv, pattern 2; Em7♭5=ii°, pattern 7; A7=V, pattern 3*; Dm=i, pattern 6.

Exercise 7: E♭m7=i, pattern 6; G♭maj7=III, pattern 1; A♭m7=iv, pattern 2; B♭7=V, pattern 3*; E♭m=i, pattern 6; D♭7=VII, pattern 5; Fm7♭5=ii°, pattern 7; B♭m7=v, pattern 3.

*altered pattern, with major third of V chord

The Melodic Minor Scale

15

Background

Besides major and natural minor, there are several other scale types a player needs to know and use for analyzing key centers. The *melodic minor scale,* or *jazz minor scale,* is one of these. (The harmonic minor scale, presented in the following chapter, is another). In jazz improvisation, selected modes of the melodic minor scale are commonly used to add some interesting scale sounds, rather than relying only on the major scale modes. In some cases, these modes of melodic minor provide solutions to chords that are not diatonic to the key and which contain alterations or extensions.

Harmonizing the Melodic Minor Scale

The melodic minor scale has half steps located between scale degrees 2–3 and 7–8. Another way to look at it is that melodic minor is like a major scale but with a flatted (minor) third. Exercise 1 shows the A melodic minor scale in first-finger diatonic and fourth-finger diatonic fingering patterns.

First-Finger Diatonic (minor)	Fourth-Finger Diatonic (minor)

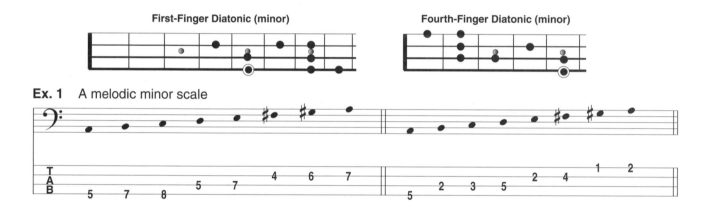

Ex. 1 A melodic minor scale

Harmonizing the melodic minor scale into seventh chords produces two new chord types. The tonic chord is a minor triad with a *major* seventh on top, written with the chord symbol "m(maj7)." The other new chord is found on the third pitch of the scale. The III chord is a major seventh with a raised fifth, or "maj7♯5." The staff below shows the harmonized A melodic minor scale.

Ex. 2 A melodic minor, harmonized in seventh chords

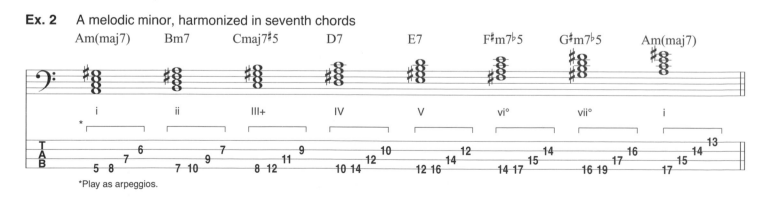

*Play as arpeggios.

50

The melodic minor scale is one of the family of minor scales, which includes natural minor, the Dorian mode, minor pentatonic, etc. However, melodic minor differs somewhat from the natural minor scale and other modes in that the player may see sharps and flats mixed together on the staff. This is quite normal and should not cause concern. A basic rule to follow is to never mix sharps and flats when the music is based on a major scale or any of the related modes. But outside of this situation, sharps and flats may be combined freely.

Notice how the G melodic minor scale below uses the key signature of G natural minor, and then accidentals are applied to create the proper half and whole step intervals. Harmonize the scale into seventh chords, labeling each chord above the staff. Then play through the arpeggio shapes shown in the diagrams below in Exercise 3.

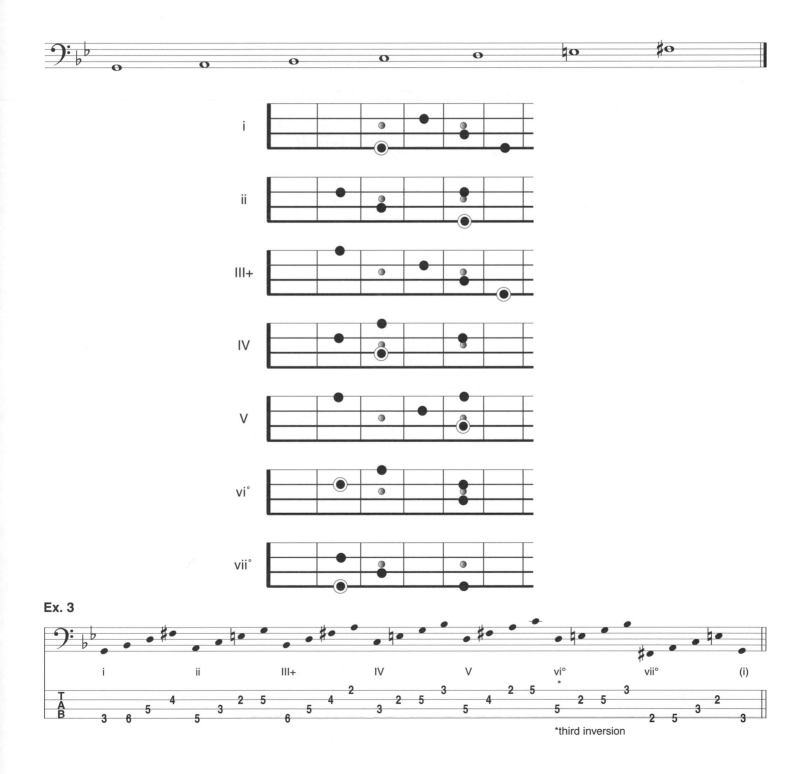

Ex. 3

*third inversion

A Melodic Minor Modes for Jazz Improvisation

As mentioned previously, several of the modes of melodic minor are commonly used in jazz improvisation. The diagrams below show the A melodic minor scale followed by its three most popular modes used in jazz and fusion—the modes starting on the fourth, sixth, and seventh steps of melodic minor. It is beyond the scope of this chapter to go into any great detail on the relationship of these modes and accompanying chords, but they are presented here to familiarize you with some of the common terms and scale types used in this style of improvising.

Ex. 4   A melodic minor scale

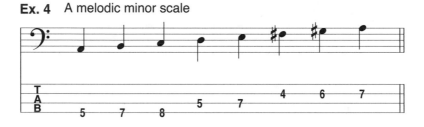

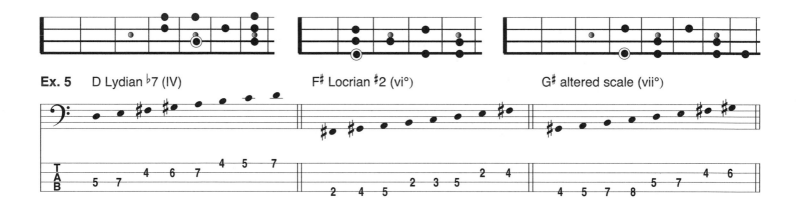

Ex. 5   D Lydian ♭7 (IV)   F♯ Locrian ♯2 (vi°)   G♯ altered scale (vii°)

The Harmonic Minor Scale

16

Background

The harmonic minor scale has been used quite extensively in rock and metal, and it also provides some solutions to chord types seen in jazz and fusion that are not found in the straight diatonic major or minor keys. Specifically, harmonic minor fits nicely with the minor ii–V cadence (Am7♭5–D7 in the key of G minor) , especially when the V7 chord contains a flatted ninth (D7♭9). In this case, both the major third and the flatted ninth are built into the harmonic minor scale, as the seventh and sixth notes of the scale. Another appealing aspect of harmonic minor is the exotic-sounding Phrygian-dominant mode, which begins on the fifth note of the scale.

Harmonizing the Harmonic Minor Scale

Below, the G harmonic minor scale is shown. Notice the augmented second (three-fret) interval between the sixth and seventh notes of the scale, which creates this scale's unusal sound.

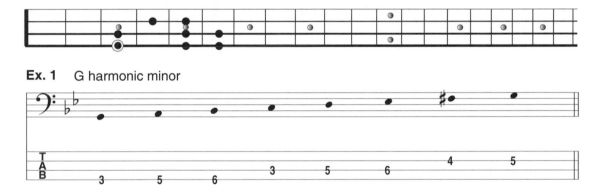

Ex. 1   G harmonic minor

Exercise 2 shows the harmonized G harmonic minor scale.

Ex. 2   G harmonic minor, harmonized in seventh chords

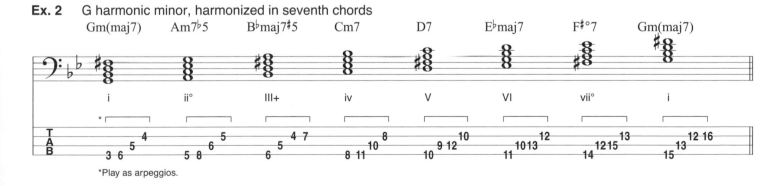

*Play as arpeggios.

Comparing the Minor Scales

The following staves compare the harmony of the harmonic and melodic minor scales to that of natural minor. Note the similarities and the differences.

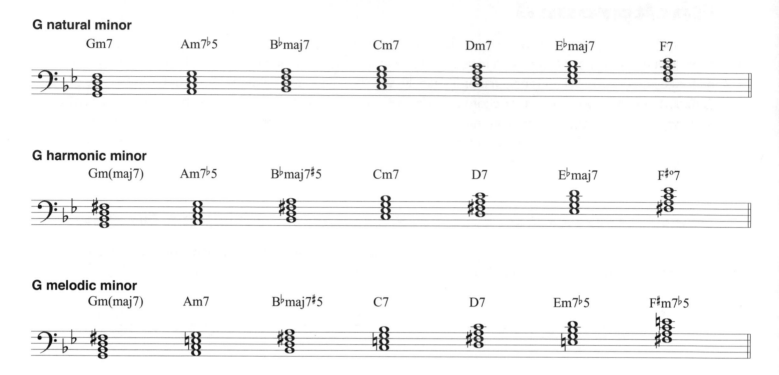

Analyzing Key Centers

17

Background

The ability to analyze diatonic information is crucial to any bassist, enabling him or her to make intelligent decisions and to realize the many playing possibilities that may exist in any given situation. Not only will a bassist then understand the various diatonic choices available, but he or she can also make decisions about how to best apply this information. This knowledge has implications in the world of songwriting and arranging as well. Below is a partial list of themes a working player needs to know fluently in order to combine the intellectual with the instinctual.

- **Key centers**. A bassist needs to gain the ability to see any key signature and immediately know the key that a song is in, as well as the areas of the neck that make playing in that key center as effortless as possible. When no key signature is available, then the player must be able to surmise the key center by looking at the chords.

- **Scales**. A bassist should know the functions of the chords in any given progression and the scale or mode that not only fits with each chord but also fits the key center. However, this information by itself is not necessarily enough to serve all purposes. In addition to major, natural minor, and the modes of these scales, the bassist must also learn the available modes and chords contained in other prominent scales in order to make good creative choices.

- **Chords**. A bassist needs to know chords (arpeggios) thoroughly, as the chord tones will always be the backbone of bass lines and solos in any style of playing. So far, this book has covered triads and seventh chords, including inversions, which will give any bassist years of useful material. In addition, the bassist will need to master the available extensions and alterations in order to create more melodic material and to learn what chord substitutions are available and useful in any given situation.

In this chapter, we will focus on analyzing chords to determine both key center and chord function as well as the accompanying scales, or modal patterns.

Analysis

The exercises that follow mix major and minor key centers. Write in the correct key center, the Roman numeral for each chord, and the correct modal shape that accompanies each chord and fits with the key center. The first example, below, has been done for you.

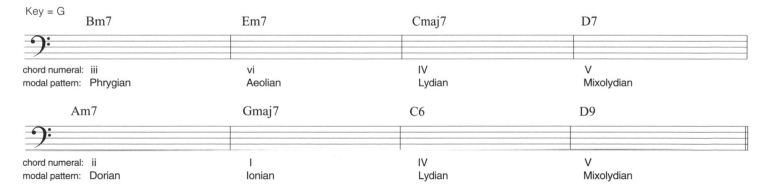

Key = G			
Bm7	Em7	Cmaj7	D7

chord numeral: iii / vi / IV / V
modal pattern: Phrygian / Aeolian / Lydian / Mixolydian

Am7	Gmaj7	C6	D9

chord numeral: ii / I / IV / V
modal pattern: Dorian / Ionian / Lydian / Mixolydian

Ex. 1

Key =   C#m7   F#m7   C#m7

chord numeral: _____   _____   _____   _____
modal pattern: _____   _____   _____   _____

Ex. 2

Key =   Fm7   Bbm7   Eb7   Fm9

chord numeral: _____   _____   _____   _____
modal pattern: _____   _____   _____   _____

Gm7b5   C7b9   Fm   Dbmaj7

chord numeral: _____   _____   _____   _____
modal pattern: _____   _____   _____   _____

Ex. 3

Key =   Bb   Gm   Cm9   F7   Dm7   Gm7   Cm7   F7

chord numeral: _____   _____   _____   _____   _____   _____   _____   _____
modal pattern: _____   _____   _____   _____   _____   _____   _____   _____

Ex. 4

Key =   C7   Dm7   C   Dm13

chord numeral: _____   _____   _____   _____
modal pattern: _____   _____   _____   _____

Gm7   F   A7b9   D5

chord numeral: _____   _____   _____   _____
modal pattern: _____   _____   _____   _____

Ex. 5

Key =   E   G#m   A5   B9   C#m   B   Emaj13

chord numeral: _____   _____   _____   _____   _____   _____   _____
modal pattern: _____   _____   _____   _____   _____   _____   _____

D#m7b5   G#9   C#m11   F#m   B7   C#m

chord numeral: _____   _____   _____   _____   _____   _____
modal pattern: _____   _____   _____   _____   _____   _____

Answers:

Exercise 1: *Key=C#m. C#m7=i(Aeolian), F#m7=iv(Dorian), B7=VII(Mixolydian), C#m7=i(Aeolian).*

Exercise 2: *Key=Fm. Fm7=i(Aeolian), Bb m7=iv(Dorian), Eb 7=VII(Mixolydian,) Fm9=i(Aeolian), Gm7b 5=ii°(Locrian),*
C7b 9=V(Phrygian-dominant), Fm=i(Aeolian), Db maj7=VI(Lydian).*

Exercise 3: *Key=Bb . Bb =I(Ionian), Gm=vi(Aeolian), Cm9=ii(Dorian), F7=V(Mixolydian), Dm7=iii(Phrygian), Gm7=vi(Aeolian),*
Cm7=ii(Dorian), F7=V(Mixolydian).

Exercise 4: *Key=Dm. C7=VII(Mixolydian), Dm7=i(Aeolian), C=VII(Mixolydian), Dm13=i(Aeolian), Gm7=iv(Dorian),*
F=III(Ionian), A7b 9=V(Phrygian-dominant), D5=i(Aeolian).*

Exercise 5: *Key=E. E=I(Ionian) G#m=iii(Phrygian), A5=IV(Lydian), B9=V(Mixolydian), C#m=vi(Aeolian), B=V(Mixolydian)*
Emaj13=I(Ionian), D#m7b 5=vii°(Locrian), [Key modulates to relative minor, C#minor] G#9=V(Phrygian-dominant),*
C#m11=i(Aeolian), F#m=iv(Dorian), B7=VII(Mixolydian), C#m=i(Aeolian).

*altered Phrygian, with major third tone

Position Playing, Part I

18

Background

Position playing means that the fretting hand will, for the most part, remain semi-fixed in the area of the neck that contains the majority of notes in a song. There are several considerations to be aware of when selecting such a position, and the right decision may depend on the situation—for example, one position may be preferred for live playing while another position may be better suited for recording. Tone is another big consideration when selecting a position and fingering.

Because the vast majority of music is based on the major scale, it is imperative to master this scale along with its harmonic implications. There are many possible major scale fingerings, but the most common and economical fingerings for position playing are illustrated below.

Common Major Scale Fingerings for Position Playing

Below, the fretboard patterns for the G major scale in second-finger diatonic are shown for four-string, five-string, and six-string bass. Play up and down through the scale patterns for the appropriate instrument (whichever you are playing) using the fingering numbers shown.

Ex. 1

G Major Scale, Second-Finger Diatonic

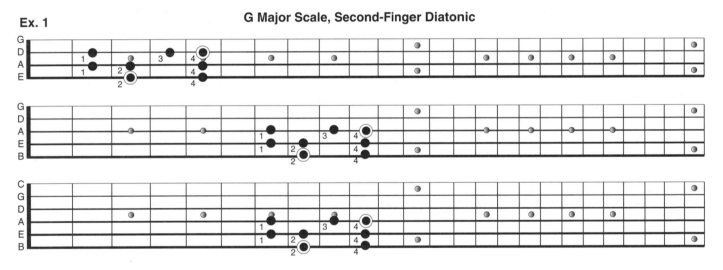

The next set of diagrams illustrate the completed position, with additional notes from the major scale.

Ex. 2

G Major Scale, Second-Finger Diatonic (Extended)

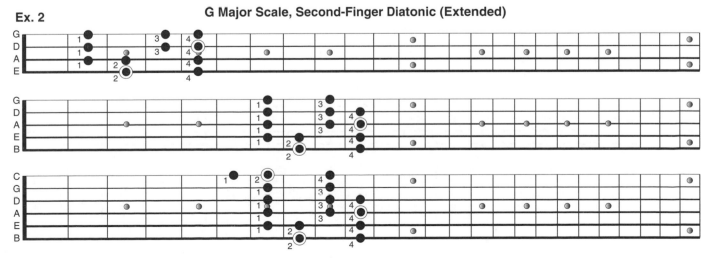

The fourth-finger diatonic pattern is shown below for the A major scale on four-string, five-string, and six-string instruments.

Ex. 3

A Major Scale, Fourth Finger Diatonic

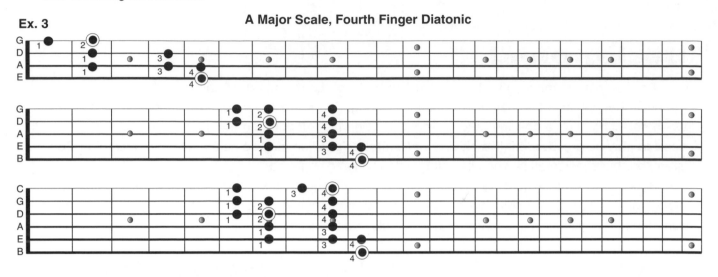

The next set of diagrams illustrate the completed position, with additional notes from the major scale.

Ex. 4

A Major Scale, Fourth-Finger Diatonic (Extended)

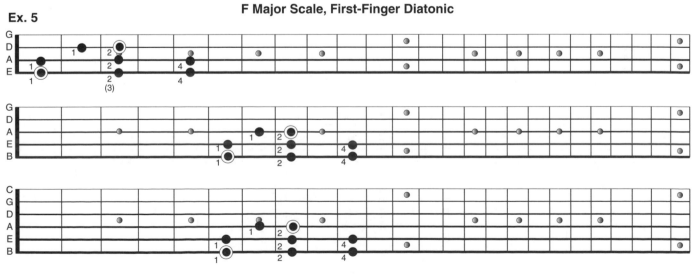

The first-finger diatonic pattern is shown below for the F major scale on four-string, five-string, and six-string instruments. Play through the scale patterns for the appropriate instrument.

Ex. 5

F Major Scale, First-Finger Diatonic

The next set of diagrams illustrate the completed position, with additional notes from the major scale.

F Major Scale, First-Finger Diatonic (Extended)

Ex. 6

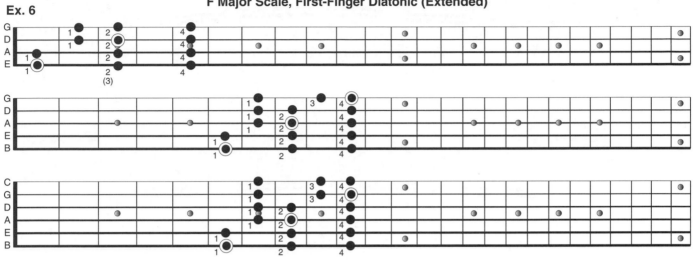

Interval Exercises

We will now play sequenced, diatonic, simple intervals (thirds through the octave) in each pattern. The pattern from Exercise 6 (four-string bass) is shown below in Exercises 7-12. Extend each sequence appropriately if you are playing a five- or six-string instrument.

Ex. 7   F major scale, in thirds

Ex. 8   F major scale, in fourths

Ex. 9   F major scale, in fifths

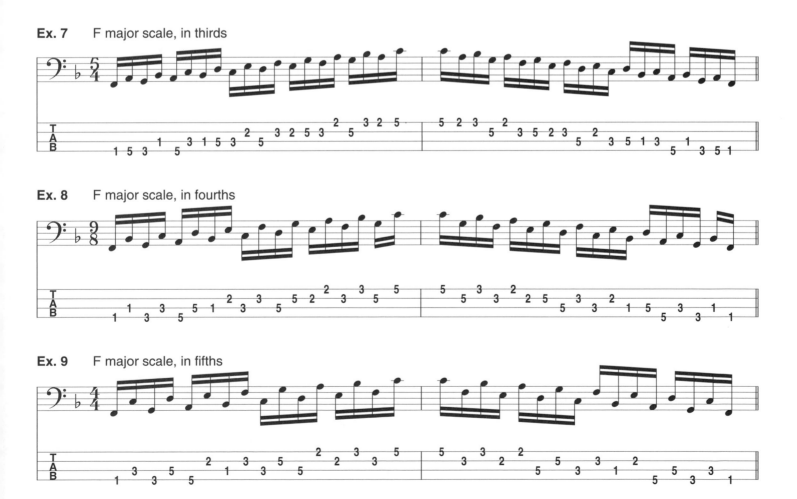

Ex. 10   F major scale, in sixths

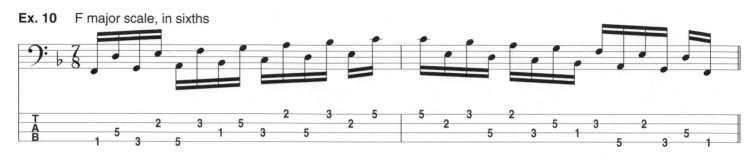

Ex. 11   F major scale, in sevenths

Ex. 112   F major scale, in octaves

Continue in this way, applying the extended scale patterns from Exercises 2 and 4 to each of the intervallic sequences shown above. Then apply this interval exercise to other major keys as well.

Position Playing, Part II

19

Background

In the previous chapter, each of the major scale patterns were started from the lowest string. Of course, this is not enough to solve all harmonic situations that a player may face—the major scale patterns for position playing also need to be learned from other strings. This chapter illustrates the major scale fingerings with the tonic, or root note, on the next higher-pitched string. In this chapter, we will also cover the complete diatonic seventh chord patterns in one position and look at the basic elements to consider in composing bass lines.

More Major Scale Fingerings for Position Playing

Below, the fretboard patterns for the C major scale in second-finger diatonic are shown for four-string, five-string, and six-string bass. Play up and down through the scale patterns for the appropriate instrument (whichever you are playing) using the fingering numbers shown.

Key of C Major, Second-Finger Diatonic (Extended)

Ex. 1

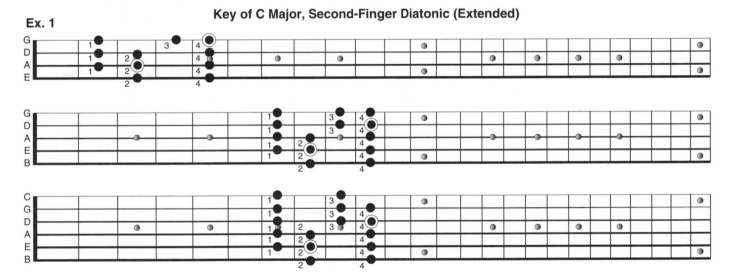

The next set of neck diagrams illustrates the D major scale in fourth-finger diatonic patterns.

Key of D Major, Fourth-Finger Diatonic (Extended)

Ex. 2

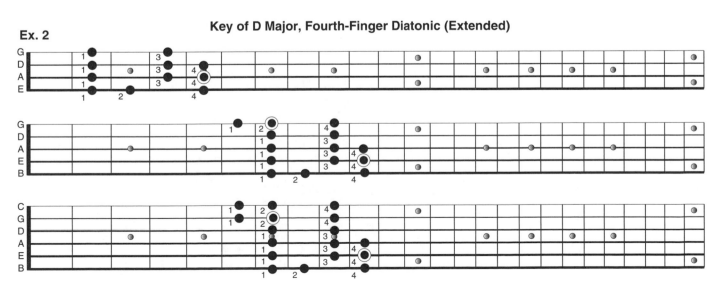

Exercise 3 shows the B♭ major scale in first-finger diatonic patterns.

Key of B♭ Major, First-Finger Diatonic (Extended)

Ex. 3

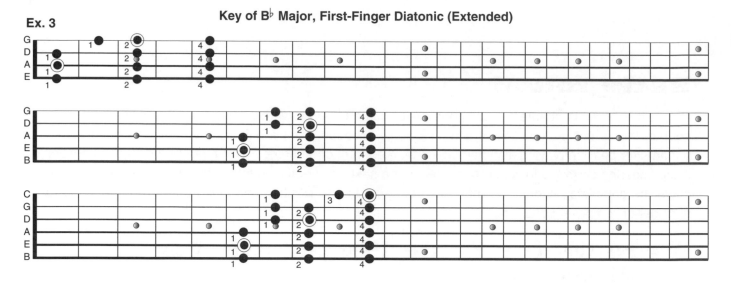

Diatonic Seventh Chords

It is important to learn the chord tones for each diatonic chord as well as the entire diatonic scale in each position. This includes *all* the chord tones—both those above and below the root note. This is especially helpful when sight reading a piece of music at moderate to fast tempos, but is also useful in maintaining good positioning control over bass lines. To ensure that this knowledge is realized, it is good to practice inverting the diatonic chords.

Exercise 4 demonstrates diatonic seventh *arpeggios* from each note of the G major scale in one position. When necessary, certain chords are inverted. Also practice this exercise using all of the major scale fingering patterns learned so far.

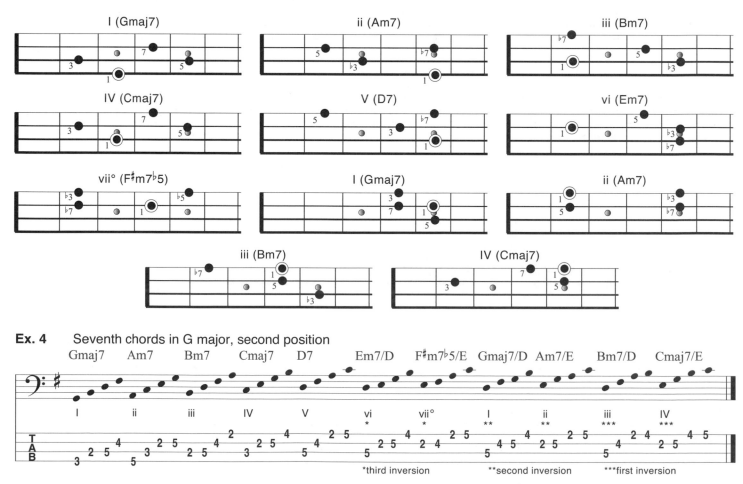

Ex. 4   Seventh chords in G major, second position

Building Bass Lines

Building good bass lines is largely a matter of deciding which notes work well over the chords of a song. Therefore, we will begin with scales. The next aspect to consider will be rhythm.

Scales

There are many choices of scales to pick from, but more often than not it is the common scales that will sound the best—especially in modern music. Two of the most common and universally recognized scales are the *major pentatonic* and the *minor pentatonic.* These are used in most forms of music including blues, rock, country and western, jazz, etc.

The pentatonic scales each contain the notes of a triad, plus two additional notes. Exercise 5 demonstrates the C major pentatonic and C minor pentatonic scales.

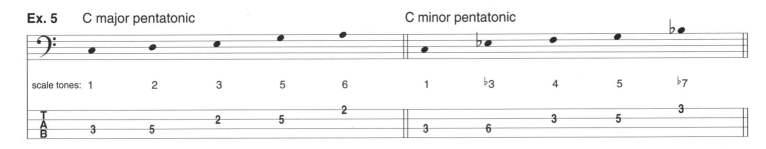

Rhythm

One of the most common rhythms to have influenced popular music for the last half century is the *clave beat.* The clave beat has its roots in Latin music but has been adapted to much rock and popular music, becoming a signature for many American artists such as Elvis Presley and Bo Diddely as well as English artists such as the Rolling Stones. The application of the clave beat guarantees rhythmic excitement in popular music, just as it has done for Latin "salsa" music.

The clave beat is commonly seen in two forms: the "forward clave" and the "reverse clave."

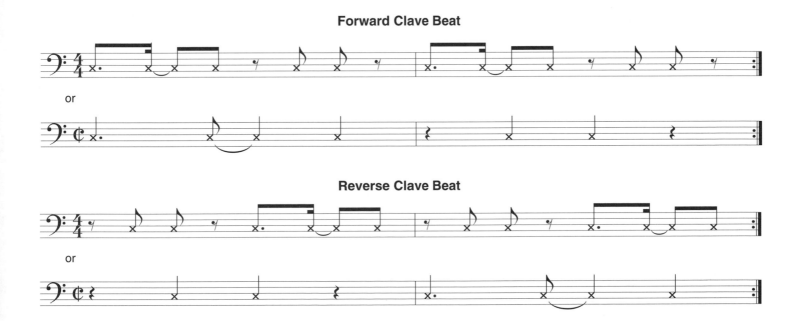

Application

Below, a bass line is shown using the A major pentatonic scale and the forward clave beat. Practice this until you are familiar with the basic pattern and rhythm.

Ex. 6

Now write out your own bass line using similar ideas for the progression below. Be sure to adapt your bass line appropriately for the chord changes. (Hint: Try applying the minor pentatonic scale over the minor chords.)

Ex. 7

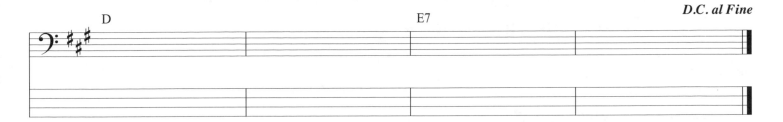

Here is another similar bass line, this time in the key of G.

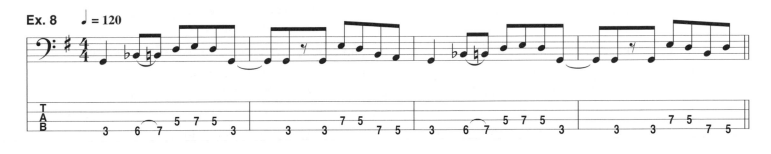

Write out another bass line for the following progression.

20 Moving Outside the Diatonic Key

Background

Knowing the notes of a key center in various positions is invaluable. However, this knowledge alone will not be enough to handle every situation. There need to be some systems in place to deal with things that are not diatonic to a key, such as *modal interchange, tritone substitution, secondary dominants,* and more.

To handle such events and yet stay within the diatonic framework, a chromatic approach is necessary. On a four-string bass, in one position, the player has access to all notes within any four-fret area of the neck. Therefore, the addition of a single fret (on each string) to the second-finger diatonic fingering pattern will provide the means to adapt to any non-diatonic situation and still maintain the same fingering position. The following exercises are designed to prepare the player for just these kind of events.

Chromatic Major Seventh Arpeggios

Exercise 1 moves major seventh arpeggios up chromatically in one position of the neck.

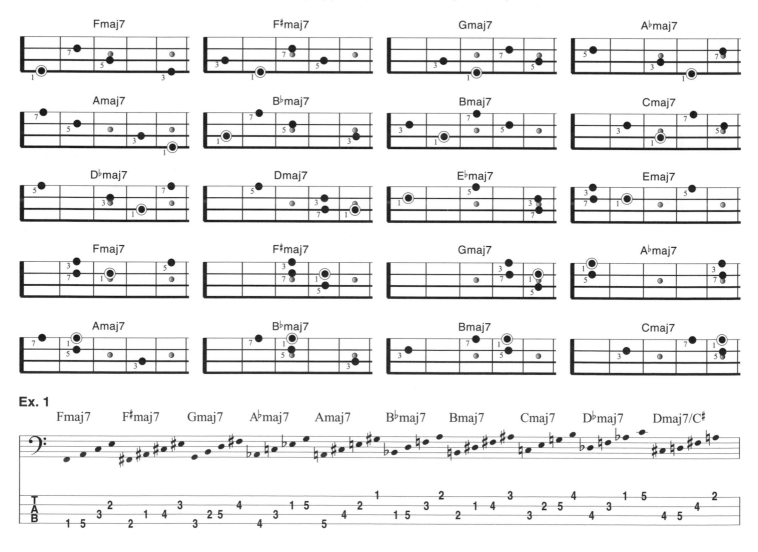

Ex. 1

66

Chapter 20

Diatonic Warm-Up

Exercise 2 moves through the diatonic arpeggios in the key of G major, in one position (except for the high E note).

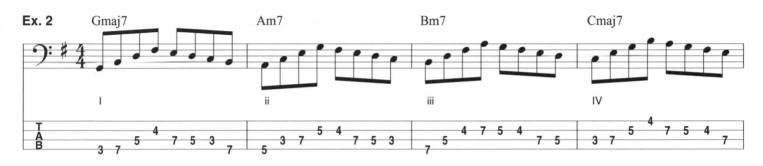

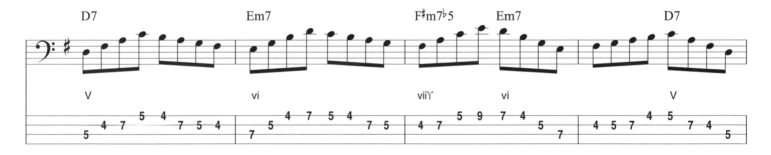

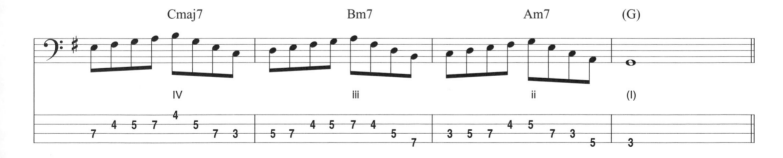

Application

Exercise 3 is a tune in the key of G. Look for the non-diatonic notes.

Ex. 3

Walking Bass Lines, Part I

21

Background

The goal of a good walking bass line is to outline, or define, the harmony of the song for the listener. This could include redefining the entire key center through the use of modes or scales, or playing each individual chord change in a piece of music. The decision of which approach to pursue depends on the type of song played. The focus of this chapter is on dealing with chord changes.

In many cases, playing the notes of the particular chord or the appropriate scale is sufficient, but in some styles a more "musical" or melodic approach is needed.

Voice Leading

To create a more melodic-sounding bass line, one must learn to resolve to a note other than the root note of each chord. In a general way, this mimics what happens in the melody of songs, although the melody usually contains a more narrow range of notes.

The walking bass line examples here emphasize the use of arpeggios to spell out each chord clearly and minimize any harmonic ambiguity. Below, each chord moves to the next by way of the nearest chord tone of the next change.

Exercise 4 shows a more complete progression using voice leading.

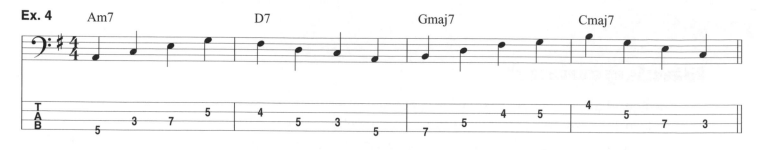

Exercise 5 shows how this same concept may be applied to a bass solo.

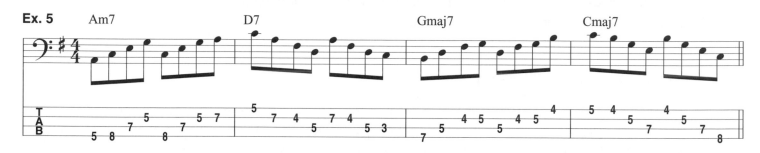

Note: In many cases, starting on the seventh of the chord—though theoretically correct—may not produce the desired results. Using the seventh (or any higher extensions of the chord) will sound more suitable in the higher octaves.

Chord Substitution

To enhance bass lines and solos, chord substitution may be used to strengthen the overall sound. The simplest place to start with chord substitution is with the dominant (V) chord because a substitute chord placed here will help propel the progression toward the next chord, without changing its function. Two of the most basic substitutions for the dominant seventh chord are illustrated below.

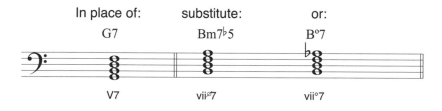

The decision of which substitution to use will often be determined by the context of the chord progression. The most common resolution contains a m7♭5 chord resolving down a fifth. It is also quite common to find a diminished seventh chord resolving up a half step. Both are shown below in Exercise 6.

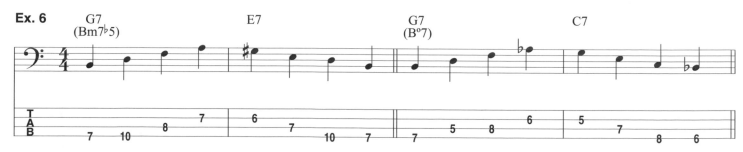

Chapter 21

Application

Exercise 7 shows a walking bass line in arpeggios, using voice leading to smoothly connect each measure.

Exercise 8 shows the same basic progression with chord substitutes.

22 Walking Bass Lines, Part II

Background

The beats of a measure can be thought of as having strong and weak points within them. In 4/4, beats 1 and 3 of each measure are considered the strong beats, and are often therefore the location of chord tones. Beats 2 and 4 are the weak beats of each measure. Ironically, it is the weak beats that provide some of the most creative points in a bass line or solo, as the player is generally more free to experiment here without undermining the defined harmonic structure.

Strong and Weak Beats

The following examples demonstrate some of the options available for altering the weak beats of the measure to create more interesting bass lines.

Ex. 1   Using scale tones

Ex. 2   Approach tones, from 1/2 step below

Ex. 3   Approach tones, from 1/2 step above

Ex. 4   Octave displacement

The next exercise demonstrates the above techniques in a twelve-bar blues progression.

Now write your own bass line for the same twelve-bar blues progression, using the same techniques for altering the weak beats.

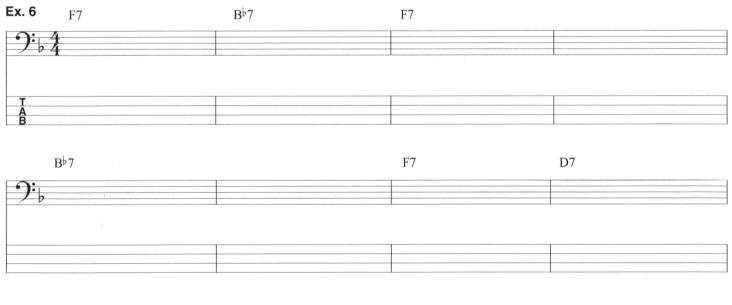

More Chord Substitution

Tritone Substitution

The *tritone substitute* is a chord substitution wherein the dominant chord (V7) is substituted with another dominant chord a diminished fifth interval away. These two chords can substitute for each other because the two most important chord tones—the third and the seventh—appear in both chords but in reversed roles. The use of the tritone substitute obligates the user to resolve to an "intended" tonic and thus makes the tritone completely interchangeable.

Common Dominant Substitutions

The following figure demonstrates several other common dominant chord substitutes. Some of the following chords are considered "legitimate" substitutes while others can be referred to as "contextual" substitutes.

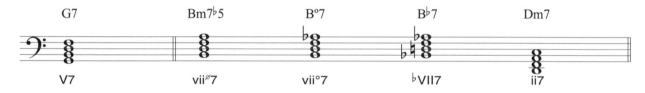

Application

The following exercise applies substitute chords to the previous twelve-bar progression.

Write out a bass line using weak beat alterations and dominant chord substitutes.

Turnarounds

23

Background

A *turnaround* is the ending portion of a progression, but not the ending of a song. The turnaround propels the listener back to the beginning of the progression or the top of the song. To accomplish this, the turnaround contains one or more dissonant chords which then resolve into the beginning of the next verse or chorus. In many cases, this is done by simply applying the V7 chord and returning to the top of the song.

What is needed by the bassist—whether accompanist or soloist—is a thorough knowledge of the options available for the turnaround, using harmony as the vehicle. In improvisation, the turnaround demands special attention as it is a crucial link in maintaining and building continuity in a solo, through repeating choruses; the soloist can use the turnaround as a platform in which to reach another, higher "plateau" in a solo.

Common Turnarounds

This basic turnaround progression is probably the most common. For the improviser, the choice would be to play off the V chord, or use a V chord substitute.

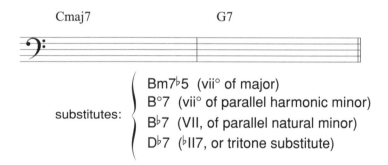

The next two turnaround progressions are more common to jazz standards and ballads. A typical walking bass line has been applied to each.

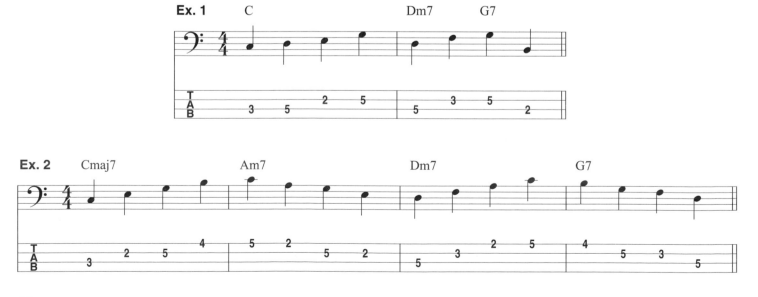

Chapter 23

Exercise 3 is a variation on the previous progression. In the right context, this progression could replace the previous one.

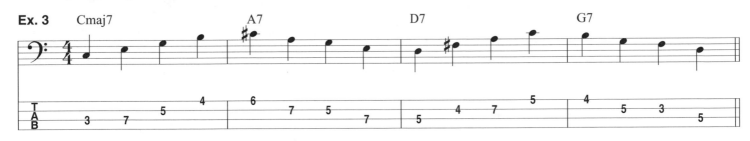

This progression is probably the quintessential turnaround progression. Write out some alternative progressions using chord substitutes. Some sample alternatives are shown below.

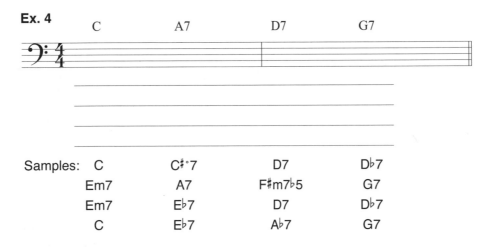

Samples:	C	C#°7	D7	D♭7
	Em7	A7	F#m7♭5	G7
	Em7	E♭7	D7	D♭7
	C	E♭7	A♭7	G7

Application

The following twelve-bar progressions include chord substitutes. In particular, notice the substitution on the turnarounds.

Ex. 6

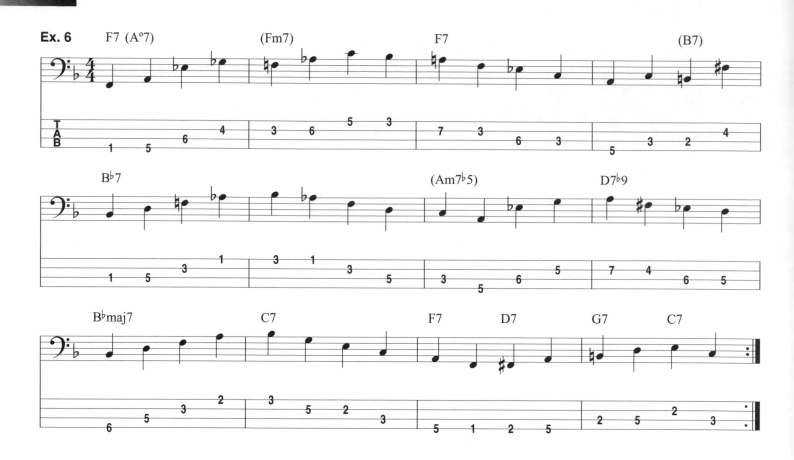

Now write out and play a walking bass line or solo over the basic twelve-bar progression using chord substitutes as in the previous examples. In particular, use dominant chord substitutes on the turnaround. Cross out and replace the chord symbols as necessary.

Ex. 7

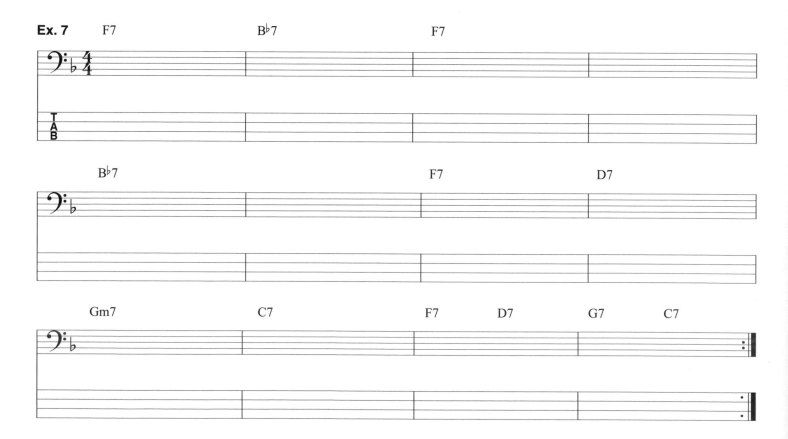

Arpeggios

24

Background

This chapter is devoted to playing arpeggios over the entire fretboard. Each section covers a different chord type, in various keys, and utilizes an ascending sequence. Chord tones that lie below the starting root are also included in the exercises. Fingerings are oriented around the previously learned diatonic fingering patterns, with emphasis on the locations of the tonic note. Also, each chord fingering is presented within the context of its common diatonic function. So, for example, the root of a minor seven flat five chord would be played by the third finger (as its function is that of a ii° chord in a minor key) or by the first finger (as its function is also that of a vii° chord in a major key).

Major Triads and Major Sevenths

The following six exercises move up the neck in sequenced major triads and major seventh arpeggios in the keys of C major, D major, and G major.

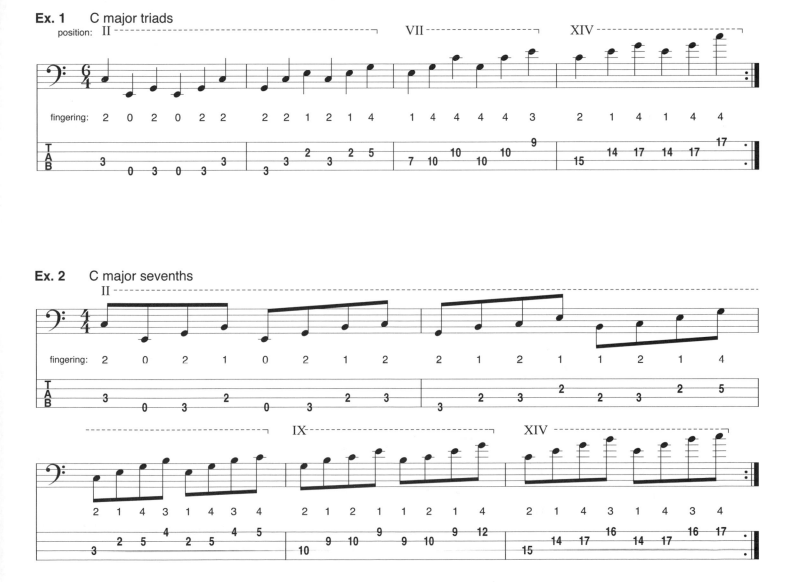

Ex. 1   C major triads

Ex. 2   C major sevenths

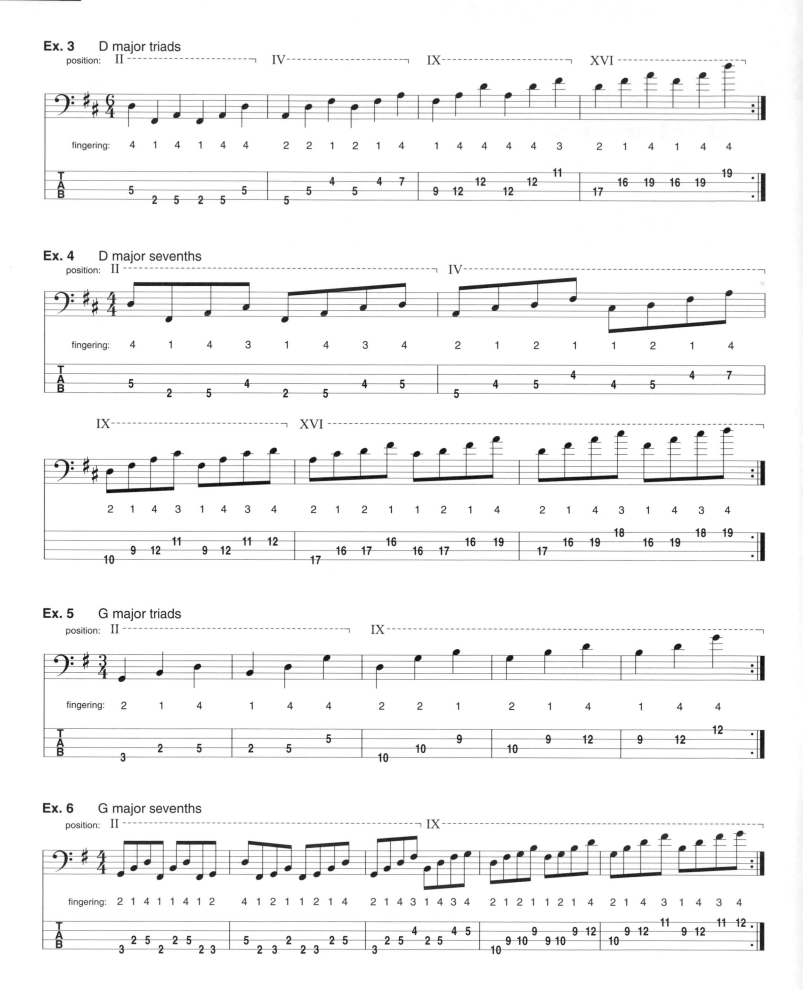

Ex. 3   D major triads

Ex. 4   D major sevenths

Ex. 5   G major triads

Ex. 6   G major sevenths

The next exercise applies triads to the chords of a 12-bar progression in G major.

Ex. 7

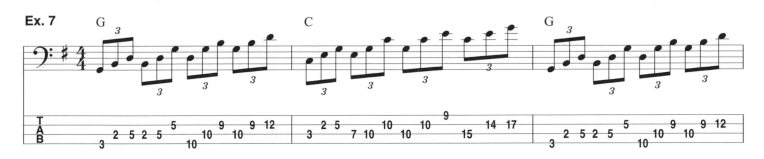

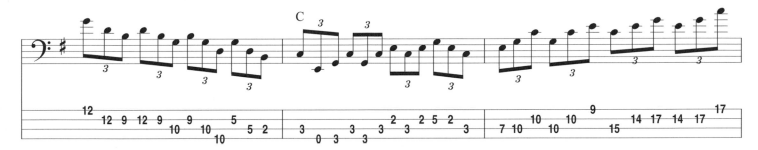

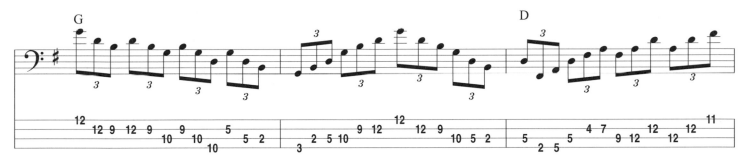

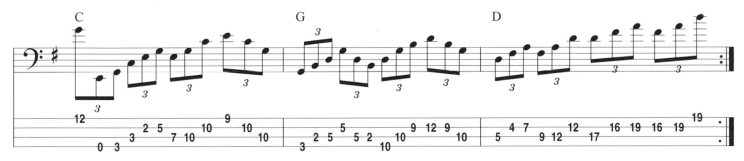

Now alter the sequence of notes played in each arpeggio so that the last note of each measure connects to the first note of the next measure using the principle of voice leading. You may also use seventh arpeggios

Ex. 8

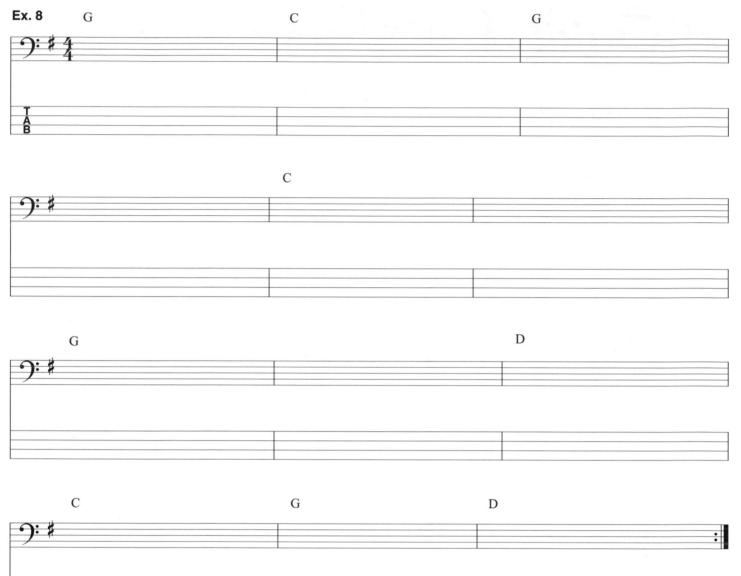

Dominant Sevenths

The next five exercises use various dominant seventh chord types, sequenced up the neck. The dominant seventh fingerings are very similar to the major seventh fingerings. The shifts will generally be the same, except for some small changes in fingering required by the flatted seventh tone.

Ex. 9

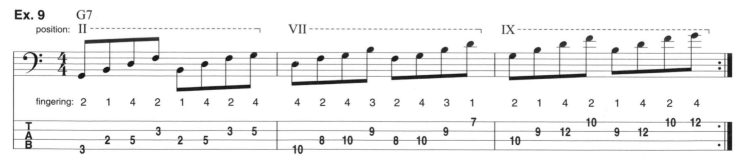

Minor Sevenths

The next four exercises use various minor seventh chord types, sequenced up the neck. The minor seventh chord is presented as a i chord (first-finger diatonic and fourth-finger diatonic) in minor keys. These fingerings will also cover the diatonic functions of the minor seventh chord in major keys as well (as ii, iii, and vi). The shifts will generally remain the same.

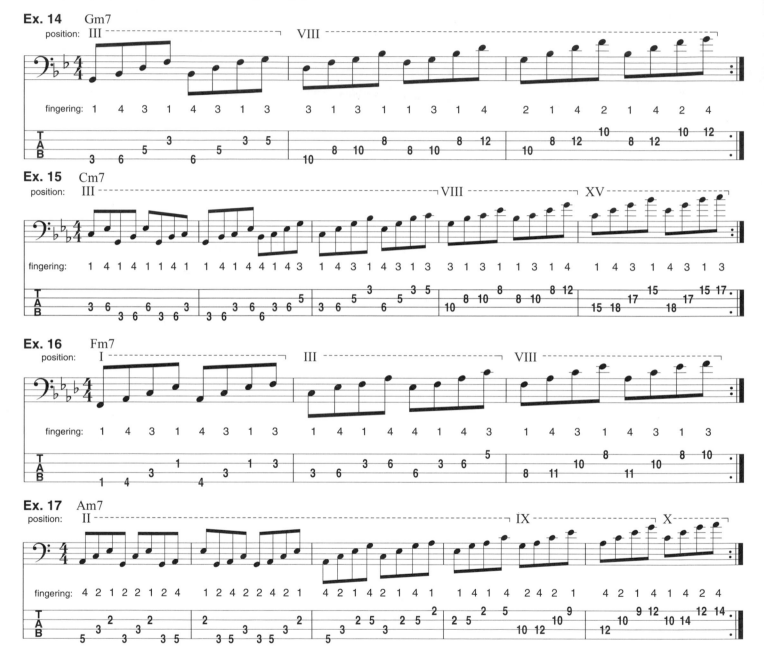

Minor Seven Flat Fives and Diminished Sevenths

The next three exercises use minor seven flat five and fully diminished seventh chord types, sequenced up the neck. The minor seven flat five chord is treated diatonically as the ii° chord in a minor key or the vii° chord in a major key, so the arpeggio begins from the third finger and the first finger, respectively. The diminished seventh is treated in exactly the same way because these starting fingers (1 and 3) give access to all the basic chord tones without any shifting.

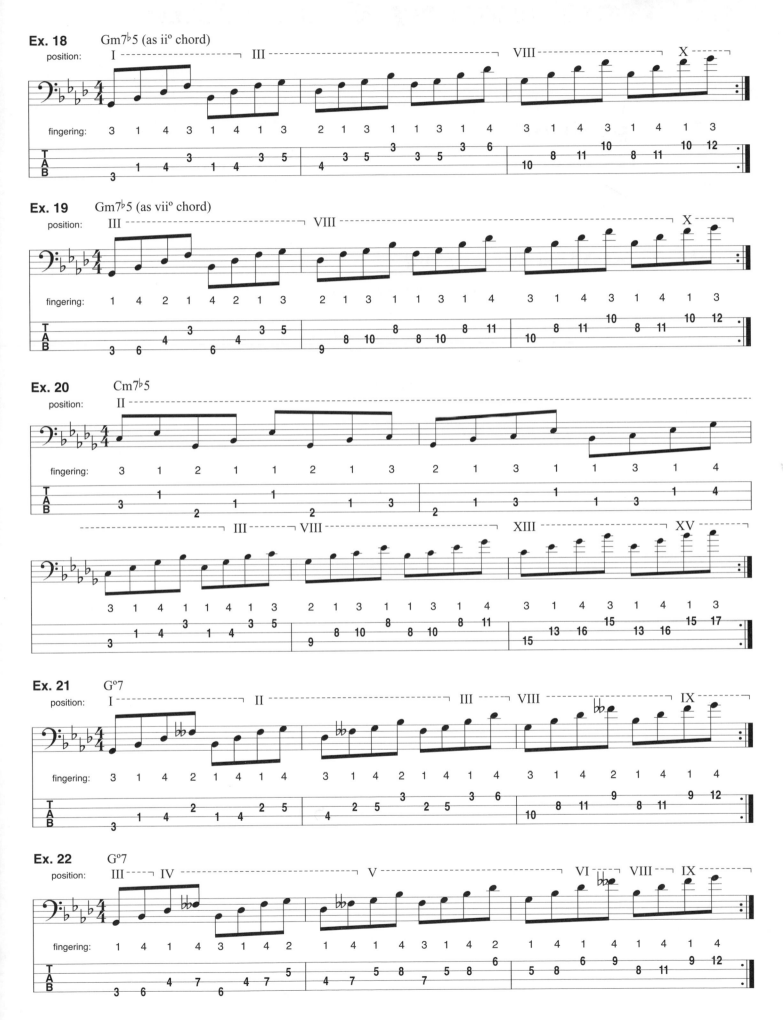

Background

Now it's time to apply everything you have learned. This chapter features two songs, outlined in progression-form only. Create your own bass line using any and all of the ideas shown in this book, then practice and perform it.

Horizontal Playing

"Horizontal" playing refers to focusing on the melodic aspect of a bass line. This song is a study in using scales as the main emphasis in creating a bass line over a single chord for varying lengths of time. Phrasing is the key to keeping both the listener and the group centered and focused on the form. Another problem to solve is in applying a V7–i sound to the phrasing.

Ex. 1

Song 1

Chapter 25

A   Dm7

Horizontal and Vertical Playing

"Vertical" playing refers to focusing on the harmonic (chordal) aspect of a bass line. This song contains both a vertical approach (in the A section, or verse) and a horizontal approach (in the B section, or bridge). Create a walking bass line in quarter notes, applying various harmonic concepts learned previously such as half-step approach tones, voice leading, octave displacement, etc. Also apply chord substitutes to reharmonize sections of the song as well.

Song 2

Ex. 2

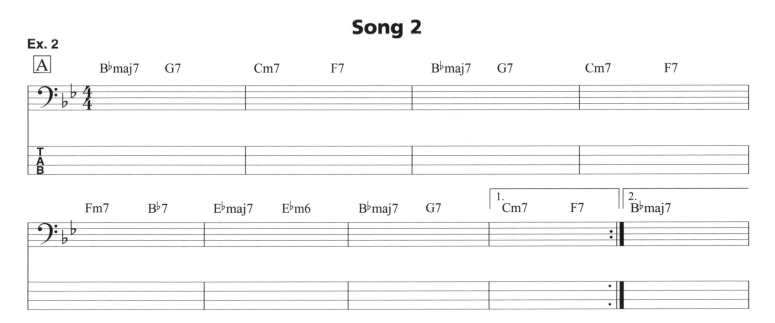

B | D7 | | G7 |

C7 | | F7 |

A | B♭maj7 G7 | Cm7 F7 | B♭maj7 G7 | Cm7 F7 |

Fm7 B♭7 | E♭maj7 E♭m6 | B♭maj7 G7 | B♭maj7 |